The Mentor's Companion

The Mentor's Companion

A GUIDE TO GOOD MENTORING PRACTICE

Rhianon Washington

UNIVERSITY OF WALES PRESS
2018

© Rhianon Washington, 2018

All rights reserved. No part of this book may be reproduced in any material form (including photocopying or storing it in any medium by electronic means and whether or not transiently or incidentally to some other use of this publication) without the written permission of the copyright owner. Applications for the copyright owner's written permission to reproduce any part of this publication should be addressed to the University of Wales Press, 10 Columbus Walk, Brigantine Place, Cardiff CF10 4UP.

www.uwp.co.uk

British Library CIP Data

A catalogue record for this book is available from the British Library

ISBN   978-1-78683-184-2
eISBN   978-1-78683-185-9

The right of Rhianon Washington to be identified as author of this work has been asserted in accordance with sections 77 and 79 of the Copyright, Designs and Patents Act 1988.

Designed and typeset by Chris Bell, cbdesign
Printed by CPI Antony Rowe, Melksham

For David

We cannot change the world around us only our reaction to it
And through that reaction we can influence others
Mentoring fosters a level of emotional intelligence that can enhance that process

Contents

Preface	ix
chapter 1 What is Mentoring?	1
chapter 2 Mentoring Skills: the Building Blocks	17
chapter 3 Mentoring Models	37
chapter 4 Toxic Mentoring	51
chapter 5 Mentoring Schemes	63
chapter 6 Distal Mentoring	81
Afterword	105
References	107
Bibliography	115
Index	123

Preface

Whether you are new to mentoring or a seasoned practitioner, common challenges confront both novice and proficient alike. *The Mentor's Companion* explores these challenges and how they can be overcome.

Mentoring is a process inherent to human activity. We can all point to instances in our personal lives of being mentored or acting as a mentor even if we do not label it as such:

- the family member guiding the young through adolescence and beyond
- the inspirational tutor who instils a desire for learning and self-improvement
- the supportive friend helping to deal with disappointments or difficult situations
- the motivational captain or coach on the sports field looking to get the best out of their players

It is a logical progression therefore to embrace this basic nurturing instinct and harness it in pursuit of personal, professional and organisational development. *The Mentor's Companion* explains the essential processes, the skills and techniques required to become a proficient mentor and how to reduce the risk of common mentoring pitfalls. The author draws on knowledge acquired through doctoral research and experience gained from training mentors and mentees in business, public services and higher education, from small schemes to major regional operations for over ten years.

The Mentor's Companion offers examples and techniques to ensure good mentoring practice, that is to say, effective mentoring that illuminates, inspires and supports. The book tells a progressive story, working from the elementary foundations of mentoring meaning and purpose, to a more intricate examination of its principles and applied mechanisms.

About mentoring

The word 'mentor' has its origins in Ancient Greek literature with an early reference in Homer's 'The Odyssey' which chronicles the protagonist Odysseus' journey home from the Trojan Wars. While away he entrusts his realm to his friend, Mentor. Modern interpretation portrays Mentor as a wise and trusted teacher who served as a role model for Odysseus' son, Telemachus. Homer, however, presents a less complimentary picture of Mentor, as Odysseus returned to find his kingdom in turmoil. Mentor's influence on Telemachus was, in fact, over-exaggerated and quite inconsequential. He was frequently imitated by the goddess Athena, the true source of the many attributes – such as inspiration – that were later associated with him. While the epic saga's portrayal of mentoring is far removed from our current understanding of the word, the enduring image remains one associated with his name and it is often cited as the birth of mentoring. The name of Mentor has now evolved to embody the ideals of a relationship involving nurturing, advocacy and integrity, and it typifies the roles of coach, counsellor, guide, guru and teacher.

The practice of mentoring as a distinct and independent activity did not attract the attention of academics until the late 1970s, and much has been written about it in the interim. A common criticism of earlier research was that it was too anecdotal and biased to the perceived benefits (Colley, 2002). More recently, however, greater emphasis has been placed on the negative consequences of mentoring and a chapter has been dedicated to it in this book. Understanding of this toxicity and how to protect the mentoring process from it has greatly improved.

The benefits of mentoring have not gone unnoticed by civic and business leaders, giving rise to an array of organisational mentoring schemes displaying an assortment of characteristics yet all designed with a similar intent: to develop the workforce. *The Mentor's Companion* addresses the themes and issues for organisational mentoring models, serving as an aid to scheme managers. The author also introduces her own adapted model: distal mentoring, born out of research conducted on a developmental mentoring scheme.

The Mentor's Companion is intended as a functional and comprehensive guide to mentoring and particular emphasis has been afforded to its use within organisational and mentor scheme structures. There is much in the book, however, to inform and support individuals who wish to develop and utilise mentoring skills, and readers are urged to work through every chapter as there are many aspects of general mentoring in each. Mentoring should not be exclusive and the knowledge gained can only inspire a better person.

The ambition of this guide for mentors, both novice and veteran, is to serve as a friend on the mentoring journey. To attain maximum benefit from the book, readers are advised to maintain a journal to note down ideas or observations and to reflect upon personal experiences as the chapters are worked through which will act as an aide-memoire, personalise the contents and offer a souvenir of the mentoring journey.

CHAPTER 1
What is Mentoring?

No textbook can be fully functional without first giving the subject some context and clarity of meaning. The present chapter illustrates why doing that may not be so easy, and seeks to explain the nature of mentoring and its somewhat incestuous relationship with allied disciplines. It contains examples of the varied ways mentoring has been applied, and highlights other literature and studies undertaken on generic and specific aspects of mentoring. This synopsis of theories and applications aims to give a better feel for the principles that lie at the heart of mentoring as well as providing a reference source for further reading.

Spontaneous mentoring, so unwittingly prevalent in all aspects of life, is equally apparent in the workplace: the colleague willing to listen; the trusted confidante; and those with values that influence attitudes, whom we seek to emulate. Its influence can be seen in many typically supportive interactions:

- helping or guiding a colleague
- showing a new colleague the ropes
- advising on organisational politics and etiquette
- championing them or acting as an advocate
- acting as a 'sounding board'

Even in these informal contacts, reflecting on efficacy and applying structures, techniques and tools can turn everyday connections into something more powerful and productive.

Inevitably, not everyone has the good fortune to benefit from informal support structures that can act as positive influences on their lives, or is inherently blessed with a drive to be winners or leaders of the pack (in what might mistakenly be viewed as a natural selection process). Establishing a more formal, targeted approach to mentoring opens the way for those who are more reserved or unguided to release their latent potential and to level the playing field. It is in fulfilling this need that mentoring delivers its most rewarding contribution to society. Mentoring is a fluid concept. Daloz (1999: 203) writes engagingly of 'The Yoda Factor' where, so long as the 'Force' is with you, the giving of support and challenge can nurture individuals not only through periods of transformation or planning long-term career pathways, but also in dealing with the routine interactions we all regularly encounter.

In its purest and most recognised form, mentoring is an intentional, nurturing process between two individuals: the mentor and mentee. Through challenge, support and reflection, it seeks to guide and facilitate growth through professional and personal change.

Historically, mentoring was more aligned to sponsorship activities, such as apprenticeships, where an experienced employee would instruct a junior colleague within the structured framework of the apprenticeship. Over time it evolved to include other relationships, for example, between two co-equal professionals as in peer mentoring. The term 'mentoring' has been applied to a variety of specific support structures creating some bewilderment over its precise definition and meaning (explored later in this chapter). There are common features to many, but not all, forms of mentoring – for example, a pastoral intent towards the mentee, illustrating an interest in and contribution to their overall well-being. More demanding methods can also be applied, such as challenging questions, which can cause the mentee some unease but still be laced with benevolent intent.

The generic essence

Daloz (1999) describes the mentoring process as a journey for both mentor and mentee, a journey that should be transformational as the mentee gains knowledge and experience. The change is unique to each individual; what comes quite naturally for one may be challenging or completely overwhelming for others. The mentor can also be influenced, especially if challenged to overcome deep-rooted dogmatism and self-limiting beliefs. The mentor can be perceived both as a guide on this journey and as a bridge between old and new beliefs. The shifting nature of the mentor-mentee relationship is also evident; at the outset, the mentor is viewed as the authority figure, and, if successful, the mentoring process results in a more equitable connection between the two participants, with the mentee occasionally surpassing the mentor's expertise.

Mentoring models are generally facilitative, enabling and non-threatening in tone. Business-based mentoring models, however, can be more aggressive in manner and sometimes even subversive in tone when ambitions and hidden agendas come into play. This raises concerns surrounding the ethical intent and underlying motives of the mentor and mentee. A moral code needs to be applied to both roles, but especially to the mentor who is better placed to exert influence, as the name itself implies. Failure to do so may betray the whole ethos of the mentor as a wise and trusted guide.

Pascarelli (1998: 231–43) cites the 'Mentor's Creed' which represents the quintessential symbol of the mentoring experience:

> I am here for you.
> I believe in you.
> I will not let you fail.
> You have the power.

The success of mentoring is hardly a revelation if an individual is guided by a respected colleague adopting such a supportive and enabling tenet. But as a synergetic partnership it is dependent on trust carefully nurtured over a period of time and of mutual benefit to both participants.

The fact that so many people benefit from the service of a mentor through informal or even imperceptible means does not weaken the value of a more formal process. Ensuring efficacy is, however, a greater challenge particularly for the untrained mentor, naïve to the moral implications of their guidance or the benefits of reflective analysis and facilitative advice, thereby creating a higher risk of complications.

'Mentoring means such a lot, because it's very difficult to define' Colley (2003: 12). Mentors can serve as coach, counsellor and role model, encompassing many functions, and the term 'mentor' has been adopted by various professions to represent specific activities, or to alter the perspectives of established roles. There are numerous sub-modalities such as executive mentoring (exclusive to high level professionals), and business or workplace mentoring, both of which adopt generic mentoring and coaching techniques. Mentoring can also take place between equals. In co-mentoring the mentor/mentee role is interchangeable (as it is in peer mentoring within groups) as it provides mutual support, shares understanding and promotes development, as well as allowing access to useful networks (Johannessen, 2016). Even the basic concept of the mentoring relationship can be turned completely on its head. One company, seeking to inject a better understanding of the workings of the organisation into their managers, innovatively assigned them mentors drawn from junior staff, who – in this instance – were the people in the know (Greengard, 2002).

Some organisations have preferred a tailored system; the National Health Service (NHS), for example, has developed styles of support akin to mentoring (including coaching, clinical supervision and preceptorship) with overlapping elements (such as a focus on career development) and a variety of approaches (goal setting, for example). Mentoring in nursing is actually closer to supervision in style. For example, a supervision record that explores areas for development also agrees targets and the actions necessary to achieve them then formally registers achievements. Although operating independently from the appraisal process, it is, nevertheless, an extension of it. Appraisal identifies an agreed outcome while supervision examines how this outcome is achieved, and forms part of an individual's personal development plan (PDP). The PDP is linked to the requirements prescribed for each job. Preceptorship is structured supervision for newly qualified professionals designed to support them through the transitional process. All these procedures are underpinned by policies and guidelines. Within an organisation the size of the NHS, mentoring can encompass many roles and be aligned to other support mechanisms.

The characteristics required of a successful mentor, as viewed by the mentee, is a patron who cares, supports, envisages and identifies potential, inspires enthusiasm and energy while injecting experience and empathy into the relationship. Megginson, Clutterbuck, Garvey, Stokes and Garrett-Harris (2006) recognise mentoring and co-mentoring as useful learning tools in the continuance of professional development and discuss the logistics for building a relationship. They also assess the desirability of choosing a mentor external to the organisation as an individual's aspirations may extend beyond their current environment. The pros and cons of such external support are explored later in this book. Internally sourced mentors, nevertheless, still deliver significant benefits for an organisation, particularly when assimilated into the appraisal process.

The mentor can facilitate and inspire learning and development. Allowing the mentee to assume responsibility for their own learning is an empowering proposition. In 'Transformational Mentoring', Hay (1995) describes the diverse roles of a mentor as ranging from role model or advocate to simply showing a colleague the ropes. Megginson et al. (2006) separate the mentoring relationship into four roles: performance improvement, development, counselling and knowledge sharing, with the mentee driving the process. The mentor, serving as an inclusive facilitator, guides and empowers their mentee.

Murray (2001) extols the virtues of mentoring and coaching within organisations to resolve skills shortages not satisfied by the standard education system, thereby addressing a variety of needs from functional literacy to leadership skills. Faced with increasing levels of illiterate school leavers, mentoring's mounting relevance has been addressed by the Department for Education and Skills (2007) through measures such as the adjustment of school performance indicators to include basic skills.

Attempts to unequivocally categorise mentoring are therefore perplexing and, some would argue, irrelevant. Bush, Adam and Saunders (1992), for instance, contend that mentoring should avoid any simplistic labelling.

Johnson and Ridley (2008: xi) refer to mentoring as 'dynamic, reciprocal, personal relationships', and identify the outstanding mentor as someone who is 'intentional' about the role. Yet it is difficult to discern a clear, consistent definition of mentoring in general or its interrelationship with coaching, 'a concept derived from mentoring' (Garvey, 2010: 352). This lack of clarity can create misunderstanding or misalignment of mentor and mentee expectations, undesirable factors which are likely to inhibit the relationship.

The mentoring/coaching conundrum

Differences between coaching and mentoring may appear clear-cut when they operate in their purest forms at either end of the coaching/mentoring spectrum. Many practising programmes draw on techniques from both purer forms, and this hybrid approach blurs the distinction, particularly at the midpoint of this spectrum. Wallace and Gravells (2007: 10) postulated whether the length of the relationship could determine definitions, suggesting mentoring relationships were likely to last longer than a coaching attachment. Daloz (1999) supports this view likening the mentoring process to a journey, and, in pursuing the metaphor, implies the need for a map to clarify the path. The mentor, in such a scenario, could be viewed as the cartographer, driving forward and mapping uncharted areas of change.

Coaching implies a more focused, task-based approach solving specific needs or developing skills (Grant, 2003), with the capability to improve short-term performance through well-defined goals and direct feedback. Mentoring encompasses a more holistic, long-term approach (Clutterbuck, 2008), yet the developmental mentor often uses coaching tools. Mentors tend to nurture potential and deliver useful insights to their mentees while enhancing their own professional life in the process. It also aids the retention and development of talent within an organisation. Coaching can refine employee performance, increase productivity and, again, safeguard staff retention. Both mentoring and coaching facilitate and inspire development, enabling the individual to assume responsibility for their own learning. Parsloe and Leedham (2009) provide a useful reference in exploring the potential basic differences to be found between coaching and mentoring with, for example, the focus of learning being short term for coaching and long term for mentoring. Irby (2013) explores mentoring, coaching and tutoring, and concludes that of the three concepts only mentoring covers the other two as a mentor will coach and tutor, but a coach or tutor rarely mentors.

Pegg (1999) analyses the varying roles of a mentor as adviser, teacher, role model, counsellor and leader, and includes coaching as a function of a mentor's role. He portrays a mentor as a trusted, wise and credible guide who helps the individual step back from their life to identify the road best followed, and a coach as one who provides more focused support, encouraging the individual to recognise their strengths and to use them to achieve everyday goals. Harvard Business Essentials (2004: xi) simplistically describes mentoring as, 'guiding others in their personal quests for growth', distinguishing it from coaching which is viewed as, 'an activity through which managers work with subordinates to foster skills development, impart knowledge'. An array of different coaching techniques are available that offer a more customised approach, such as executive coaching, along with the relatively recent innovation, positive psychology, explored more fully later in this chapter.

Coaching and mentoring both encourage reflection through facilitation, even modifying how individuals regard themselves and their potential. This reflective facilitation can identify problems and set goals to address them. This creates a practical design with minimal interference that encourages identification and resolution of problems in a reflective manner and allows an active role in the process to be exploited. The principles of facilitation can similarly be applied to mentoring as the delivery of this help and support stimulates the mentee to manage their own development.

The assimilation of this awareness into organisational policy and strategic direction empowers both individual and business. Using techniques such as cascade coaching and transformational learning can direct and guide a business through times of change or growth.

Organisational mentoring

Employers generally recognise that their most valuable asset is the people that work for them. It is sound business sense, therefore, to make some investment in workforce development in the same way as upgrading new technologies or more efficient machinery to deliver that competitive edge. Mentoring now forms part of many organisational strategies. Formal mentoring can be incorporated within other established processes such as appraisal, although the involvement of the line manager or supervisor can impose upon the motivational dynamics of the outcome and unbalance the relationship. Conflict could arise should the manager invoke their power position, or use information gathered during a confidential mentoring encounter for their own purpose. Conversely, a line manager could perceive a threat to their position or authority from any external support provision. Clutterbuck (2004) explores the dangers of power alignments where a mentee may use the mentoring relationship to undermine their line manager, or where a mentoring network operates outside of company policy or becomes elitist – the antithesis of the ethos to which mentoring aspires. Such conflicts can be avoided provided roles and expectations of all parties are properly clarified.

Successful relationships are mentee/learner driven, but appropriate matching is vital and best mobilised by the organisation itself. In such cases, the mentor's agenda must support the tenet of mentoring: placing the mentee's needs and welfare ahead of the organisation. Weaving mentoring techniques into a job role could prevent negative or unhelpful attitudes between colleagues, whilst amplifying the skills associated with helping each other. Some even argue whether mentoring should be regarded as a distinct activity or be subsumed within another role. Debate over such demarcation is continuous and somewhat enigmatic as many of the skills utilised by a mentor can be found in other roles such as a manager. Generally, however, mentoring is regarded as a specific developmental tool and is best used as such. Therefore, a strong case remains for an independent mentor with no conflicting constraints.

There are clear organisational advantages to mentoring within a structured framework where monitoring and assessment can be applied to enhance understanding, appraisal and accountability. Monitoring may involve the sharing of information discussed within the mentoring session and can seem at odds with its confidential nature. The fact that mentees are encouraged to trust and confide in their mentor highlights a potential ethical dilemma. If we are to increase our understanding and improve the mentoring process there is a case for monitoring, provided the mentee is aware of it. However, as trust grows and the relationship becomes stronger, there is a greater probability of a mentee dropping their guard and forgetting that information may be shared. For mentoring to be truly successful, the dyad – the combined pairing of mentor and mentee – needs to support a high level of trust. This is rooted in the mentee's aims, the mentor's motivation and the organisational demands of the relationship. If there is any possible conflict for the mentor, the most appropriate solution is for the dyad to discuss it openly and without constraint within the session and finish by agreeing what may be shared in the monitoring process.

Mentoring also plays a part in dealing with social value perspectives. Programmes have been designed to address specific societal problems, such as gender inequality in the workplace, by the creation of an enabling and facilitative work environment in order to encourage an empathic working ethos. Gender inequality initiatives have included partnerships funded by the European Social Fund, such as EQUAL (EC, 2007), which sought change in the engineering, construction and ICT industries by applying mentoring techniques so as to share good practice and overcome barriers for women within non-traditional work areas. It operated in partnerships with several European organisations including Deutsche Telekom in Germany and WomenIT in Finland. Quite modest workplace initiatives can be very effective, such as the Guardian's 'Positive Action Work Placement Scheme'. Running since 2001, it has provided mentoring to over 100 individuals from ethnic minority backgrounds. Other notable projects include the Australian 'More Than a Game' youth mentoring scheme that uses sport to tackle violent extremism. There has been a proliferation of similar initiatives as the mentoring movement has gained momentum and government funding opportunities have expanded in acknowledgment of the need for proactive interventions. A formalised process can provide a framework of guidance for participants and address a range of professional and social ills.

Colley (2003) analyses engagement mentoring specifically for disaffected youth that attempts to encourage young people at risk to enter training and employment. The process, like transformative learning, promotes a shift of values (and relates directly to Bloom and Krathwohl's (1956) categorisation of the affective or intuitive self in the taxonomies of learning) by challenging existing beliefs. An assessment and explanation of institutional mentoring can be found in later chapters.

Complementary techniques

Various studies have identified particular traits, philosophies and approaches that can be exploited to supplement mentoring and all are capable of being learnt. Emotional Intelligence, resilience, mindfulness and positive psychology can all play a part in enhancing the mentoring process. The following sections explore why and how they do so.

Emotional Intelligence

Emotional Intelligence (EI) and mentoring are natural companions. Despite the proliferation of theories and interpretations of what constitutes EI, it is, in its simplest form, best described as the understanding of feelings (including your own) and recognising their triggers and reactions so they can be controlled and managed more effectively. Anger can be a very powerful emotion that alienates the brain from logical thought. For example, if your manager shouts at you an instinctive reaction may be to shout back, a response unlikely to aid your career. EI creates the space to analyse the situation, seek indications such as body language to forewarn of danger and avoid initiating the adrenalin-fuelled flight or fight response. Seeking to understand your manager's disproportionate behaviour will likely lead to an EI response; speaking calmly as the initial anger is vented allows a more rational interaction to save face as opposed to shouting back and stapling his tie to the desk for good measure.

Our brain reacts differently when we are under pressure. Under normal circumstances information is received through our five senses: sight, sound, touch, taste and smell, and then transmitted to our thalamus. The thalamus determines to which part of the brain the signals should be directed, usually the cortex, which is the conscious thinking part of our brain. During a perceived emergency, the thalamus bypasses the cortex altogether and sends the signals directly to the amygdala, which handles emotions, initiating an immediate intuitive response. The signal arrives quicker at the amygdale than to the cortex, which is handy if you're about to be engulfed by a forest fire as you will cease to take stock of the wondrous flora and fauna you had earlier admired and dive headlong into the river to avoid burning. Such instinctive knee-jerk reactions serve to protect us from imminent threat but do not always deliver an appropriate outcome, especially if you can't swim or the river is full of crocodiles. Occasionally, we also fall victim to emotional misreading where our instinctive responses are out of date. The amygdala compares what we are experiencing now with past experiences and any similarities invoke the same previous emotional response even if inappropriate to the actual situation. The old adage of counting to ten is a wise one, as one can ignore the triggered response and pause to allow the emotional impact to subside and a more rational reaction to take over. Taking some time out to analyse and recognise your own emotions assists in the more effective management of them.

Exhaustive efforts have been made to identify the specific features, factors, abilities and skills contributing to EI. While there is still no universal agreement on which components should be included, the common ones identified in salient models can be bracketed broadly into four separate but interrelated categories: well-being, self-control skills, emotional skills and social skills. The most common specific characteristics found by Furnham and Petrides (2003) were as follows:

- adaptability
- assertiveness
- emotion expression
- emotion management (others)
- emotion perception (self and others)
- emotion regulation
- impulsiveness
- relationship skills
- self-esteem
- self-motivation
- social competence
- stress management
- trait empathy
- trait happiness
- trait optimism

Proficiency in these facets generates qualities in terms of:

- emotional literacy: knowledge and understanding of one's own emotions and how they operate
- emotional fitness: trustworthiness, emotional hardiness and flexibility
- emotional depth: emotional growth and intensity
- emotional alchemy: using emotions to identify creative opportunities

Any organisational doctrine encouraging emotional expression will nurture a culture of respect, sincerity and honesty, and will harvest an emotionally intelligent workforce as a consequence. The result is a more focused and strategically effective organisation with a discernible sense of community amongst its members. Leaders possessing high EI modelling behaviours associated with emotional and social competence display the levels of integrity so crucial to successful leadership.

The five domains model (Goleman, 1995) identifies the following attributes as significant: knowing your own emotions, managing them and motivating yourself, as well as understanding other people's emotions and managing them or the relationship. EI is therefore about establishing balance and perspective and adopting a mature approach to feelings in order to be able to step back, acknowledge what you are feeling, what others are feeling, and then, crucially, to control these emotions and your responses to others so that it does not interfere with your ability to think.

The combination of EI and mentoring blends a potent mindful cocktail. Mentoring encourages mentees to take ownership for their professional development allowing mentors to take a back seat and the mentee to lead the way, while EI liberates the dyad from inhibiting feelings. The overall process instils a high level of awareness in both parties.

EI can be achieved in mentoring by working in tandem to ensure the session is imbued with respect, empathy, sincerity, positive reinforcement, effective listening, giving and receiving constructive feedback, and many of the other qualities associated with the developmental mentoring model (see chapter 3). This may appear more like the mentor's role but when the mentee adopts a similar mindset the potential for the session grows exponentially.

The mentee should come to a session to learn, develop and improve, with the mentor as an overseer to that transformation and responsible for ensuring the process is handled in a safe environment. EI helps to facilitate that while shaping transferable skills that can enhance both in all areas of life. This respect opens up a world of possibilities, and if mentor and mentee practise, reflect and refine their emotional intelligence the relationship will be all the richer.

Cherniss (2007: 432) made a connection between EI and mentoring, deducing that it influenced the quality of mentoring and is of significance to mentor and mentee alike. He quotes Brechtel's study (2004) which identified key elements that could affect the quality of mentoring, including respect and being valued, both ingredients of emotional intelligence (Goleman, 1998). Cherniss (2007) argues that the relationship between emotional intelligence and mentoring is synergetic, concluding that mentoring develops emotional competence and that those who are emotionally intelligent influence the quality of the mentoring relationship.

Mentoring's emphasis on communication skills and empathic understanding relate strongly to the factors associated with emotional intelligence. Its training encourages the mentor not merely to listen, but to do so non-judgementally and use empathy to aid understanding. Studies have also shown that emotional intelligence increases resilience

(Armstrong, Galligan and Critchley, 2011; Görgens-Ekermans and Brand, 2012) which is another aim of effective mentoring.

Resilience
Resilience, the ability to withstand or recover quickly from difficult conditions, is vital in today's working world. Higher expectations, increasingly faster communications and the ever present spectre of redundancy portray the idea that work consistently demands more from us for less. Resilience is motivation in the face of adversity that pursues self-actualization and individual strength (Arora and Rangnekar, 2014). Why are some more resilient? The same adverse event can inflict damage on one person while the other thrives. Mental toughness is thought of as a character trait, but resilience can in fact be learnt and developed. Stress does not have to be negative, it can be motivational, it is a question of balance. Latham, Locke and Fassina's High Performance Cycle (2002) recognises that sustained stress can be damaging, risking burnout while too little can lead to apathy.

Mentoring can increase resilience, which becomes stronger when the individual feels valued, feels in control, has self-efficacy and develops positive attitudes. Being the focus of supportive attention from a mentor, the mentee will feel valued, and, if the mentor allows them the space to fully participate by contributing ideas and solutions, they will also feel empowered. This has even greater significance where there is a lack of control in other areas of life. Understanding one's own strengths reaffirms self-image and respect, and, by identifying acknowledged weaknesses, we can support and bolster them accordingly. In order to establish a positive attitude, it is first necessary to challenge unhelpful thoughts.

Scenario: Rosie challenges Jasper

> *Jasper:* Henry hates me!
> *Rosie:* Does he? Hate is a strong word.
> *Jasper:* Well, he can't like me then.
> *Rosie:* Why would you think that?
> *Jasper:* He's just given me that huge project to run, I haven't got the time.
> *Rosie:* Maybe he just trusts you to deliver; I'd love a chance to prove myself.

Reflection: Taking a closer look at the language we use and evaluate it to see if it is reasonable can help promote a positive mindset. Negativity can weaken resilience and our ability to deal with stressful situations. Simply because you feel threatened does not mean that someone is a threat, it is merely a reflection of your own perception, and, through the process of critical examination, it is possible to remove that perceived threat.

Resilience-based activities can (Copeland and Peck Beins, 2005), for example, focus on developing the internal locus of control, where the mentee's perception of events are controlled and influenced by their own actions (internal locus) rather than uncontrollable circumstances or forces (external locus). Another effective resilience development tool is identifying and discussing role models who have demonstrated resilience.

The pursuit of resilience can be boosted by another closely related doctrinal approach, mindfulness.

Mindfulness
Mindfulness is being fully engaged in the present, and involves an acute awareness of self and environment in a non-judgemental way – an elevated consciousness. There are many benefits associated with being mindful, including an appreciation of your life and yourself. Mindfulness allows the challenges and trials of life to be embraced as much as its highlights (Pryce-Jones, 2010). Mentors, for example, through the use of powerful questions can stimulate cogent insights and deeper understanding in their mentees. Mentoring creates reflective space, so is a natural environment in which to identify values and focus on goals that align with them. Mindful application is more pertinent for the mentee, the focus being on self. The mentor assumes the role of facilitator, and therefore, within the session, is less likely to engage with mindfulness in order to maintain focus on being present for the mentee (Cox, 2013). However, emotional intelligence naturally aligns to mindfulness (Wells, 2016), and by utilising qualities such as compassion, the mentor can create a mindful environment. A mindful, emotionally intelligent mentor with strong self-regard and self-acceptance can exert influence on the mentee through example.

By creating this reflective space for the mentee, mentoring introduces a powerful mindful appreciation of life to this arena. It fosters understanding and harmonises competing aspects of life: work, family, friends and personal development, allowing each to flourish independently, to reduce stress and increase resilience, so ensuring that the way we live aligns to our values. Attaining this perception of self opens the way for replacing negative attitudes with more positive convictions.

Positive psychology
Positive psychology can be defined as the study of positive emotions and how they can be harnessed to improve behaviours and performance; in other words, how we can learn to be happy. Psychology's original remit was three-fold: to cure mental illness, improve normal lives and develop high talent (Seligman and Csikszentmihalyi, 2000). Positive psychology was only acknowledged as a recognised branch of psychology in the 1980s, prior to which it was regarded with little significance. Psychology's original focus was on post-war treatment of battle-weary soldiers suffering a range of psychoses. Developed by Martin

Seligman out of his experiments on the concept of optimism, he concluded that positivity could be learnt. He identified three dimensions of optimism: personal, pervasive and permanent. A pessimistic viewpoint, for example, of seeking to lose weight may be that:

- you did not try hard enough (personal)
- you failed to lose weight and therefore will fail all attempts (pervasive)
- you will never try to lose weight again (permanence)

Seligman argued that by identifying whether your response fell into one of these categories the objection could be challenged and its power removed by replacing it with a more optimistic perspective:

- the weight goal was unrealistic at this stage (personal)
- while you didn't lose weight this week you might next week (pervasive)
- you will keep trying (permanence)

Silencing the inner critic in relation to future behaviour and allowing a more optimistic voice encourages further attempts rather than merely giving up. This concept has obvious advantages and applications within professional development, and mentoring affords the perfect vehicle for this shift in attitudes. There are wider influences that can affect optimism and happiness. Pryce-Jones (2010) identified five elements: contribution, conviction, culture, commitment and confidence which, when underpinned by pride, trust, recognition and achieving potential, ensures happiness in the workplace. Realisation, however, must begin with self-awareness.

As a field in its own right, positive psychology is gaining momentum; its influence on mentoring is evident in the emergence of newer approaches such as strengths coaching that re-focuses the emphasis from what needs to be fixed to the development of the mentee's strengths, thereby building and nurturing confidence. This is particularly effective where a mentee is stuck in a negative behavioural spiral. This spiral occurs when low self-esteem influences behaviours that induce an external reaction which then feeds back into even lower self-esteem. Changing behaviour positively influences these external reactions and ultimately breaks the spiral. For example, someone fearful of speaking at a meeting may display this through hesitancy. Listeners may interpret this as a lack of knowledge casting doubt on the validity of the person's words. When audience reaction is observed by the speaker, they become even more nervous of speaking, perpetuating the negative spiral. Convincing the person to display and speak with confidence initially (even if it doesn't exist) leads to a more positive response, bolstering self-esteem and encouraging them to continue speaking. It is a clear indication that the reaction of others can have a direct effect on our self-belief and emotional well-being.

Searching out positive traits and formulating ways to reinforce and apply them empowers both individual and organisation alike: as the positivity ripples outwards, a wise manager is able to identify the individual strengths of their team, set realistic and achievable goals, and utilise them for immediate benefit.

Summary

The proliferation of mentoring models and applications can conjure a bewildering impression and explains the inability to attach a precise definable tag but does provide clear evidence that a one-size-fits-all course of action rarely satisfies all needs, particularly at organisational level. It can be seen how the central tenet of mentoring has been progressively adapted or evolved to serve a range of functions or address specific needs. This fluidity gives mentoring a depth and potency that supports both personal progression and organisational effectiveness and, in fact, any sphere of life where human activity can be enhanced.

Having addressed the broader background, we can now move on to the more specific and engaging practicalities of mentoring.

CHAPTER TIPS

When embarking on a mentoring relationship, regardless of its external aim, style or intention, the main consideration is that the dyad (the mentor and mentee) agrees their own understanding and commits to the activity. Therefore, discussions around what mentoring means to you and how the complementary techniques could be incorporated to enhance your relationship will ensure a happy outcome for you, your mentee and the organisation.

CHAPTER 2
Mentoring Skills: the Building Blocks

Common skills are found in all styles of mentoring and represent the building blocks of an effective mentoring conversation. While essentially mentor skills, they also facilitate learning for the mentee as, in a successful relationship, the mentee tends to mirror the behaviours of their role model, a transference process through which the dyad grows. The opportunity to reflect and consider how they conduct themselves also provides a development prospect for the mentor and a chance to lose some bad habits.

A key skill for mentors is knowing when to hold back advice and allow the beneficiary to formulate their own wisdom. Such facilitation is vital if an individual is to achieve self-learning. This enveloping ethos differentiates mentoring from the more directive methods of support. Establishing a mentee's needs is fundamental to a successful association and starts with finding empathy.

Empathy

The ability to understand another's emotions, known as 'cognitive empathy', can greatly enhance the mentoring process. Affective empathy – merely responding to another's emotions through, for example, mirroring (where body language is copied) – encourages initial superficial rapport but the mentee must be fully understood for the relationship to mature. Empathic skills are better accomplished by first looking at yourself. Awareness and understanding of your own biases are vital in acknowledging another's perspective as it is then far easier to put that bias aside. Imagine being that person, focus on how they may feel and be open and non-judgemental about who they are and what they want. Challenge your opinions by asking:

- Is that an assumption?
- What evidence is it based on?
- Are my own biases and preconceptions clouding my empathy?

Opening up to empathy can be easily practised and refined until it instinctively forms part of your mentoring persona. The effect on the mentee is significant and the relationship will grow more successfully and rapidly where genuine empathy is established. Always remember, insincerity is hard to hide.

In her qualitative evaluative study of a mentoring/coaching scheme, Hargreaves (2010) noted that the hope of many of the clients was to experience some control or power through the co-constructivist approach of the process. We construct learning through our knowledge, experience and reflection to increase our understanding. Co-construction is the process of building knowledge through interaction between two people. Understanding the co-construction model and applying intentional empathy to it creates the structure that drives the mentoring process. Using empathy to enhance this 'construction' is important, not merely at the outset but throughout the relationship to reinforce empathic understanding and boost the feeling of power for the mentee.

Combining constructed knowledge with an empathic mentor increases a mentee's confidence and enables better coping mechanisms. Empathy is explored in detail by Cox (2005) who uses the term 'empathic authority' to describe the power entrusted to the mentor by the mentee until sufficient rapport is secured. This is a crucial stage in the relationship as roles are established and clarified. It requires a high level of skill on behalf of the mentor, but without appropriate training and development it can increase the risk of toxicity (where mentoring breaks down or is damaged).

The layers of a mentor are onion-like, encompassing a range of stratagems, roles and identities in support of the mentee so as to promote empathic co-construction and reinforcement. The mentor then selects an appropriate line of action according to the needs of the mentee. The power of such tactics is better appreciated if we first consider the following theories.

Ego states and life roles

Transactional Analysis (Berne, 1966) is the interpretation of social interactions and the adoption of specific ego states. Berne identified three distinct ego states: Parent, Child and Adult. The Parent represents our taught understanding of life: the rules, limits and traditions, and can involve criticism, nurturing, guidance and judgement – 'You Should'. Parent behaviours are categorised in two ways: Nurturing Parent and Critical Parent. The characteristics are drawn from authority figures we have experienced in our lives. The Child state is the concept of feelings: fun-loving, creative or rebellious – 'I Want'. It is also divided into two categories: Free Child, which can be positive (as in joyful behaviour), or negative (as in anger), and Adapted Child which interacts with authority figures either through compliance or rebellion. The Adult state describes thought and is objective, factual and unemotional – 'I Think'.

This theory can be applied to everyday social interactions. By observing these interactions, it is surprising how easily the different ego states can be identified. For example, 'you must finish that project on time' – Critical Parent. Or, 'I want Friday off!' – Free Child.

Berne's ego states can also be linked to other personality characterisation such as Karpman's (1968) drama triangle that describes the roles we may adopt in interactions. Karpman identified three main life roles: Persecutor, Rescuer and Victim. The Victim may consider themselves very unlucky in life and in need of care (by the Rescuer) or control (by the Persecutor). Each role relies on the other to perpetrate the life role. When observing social interaction, it is possible to identify both these theories. For example, 'I always have to work late!' – Negative Free Child and Victim.

Observation is essential to mentoring, and understanding how people regard themselves within interactions influences the mentoring process. The mentee can be helped to transform a Critical Parent Persecutor response to an Adult ego state through awareness and reflection. It is also useful to observe your own behaviours, taking note of the roles and egos you may adopt. This enhances self-awareness, increases mentor effectiveness and develops empathic skills and capacity. Identifying and understanding the current behaviour of your mentee can, through empathic reinforcement, guide them to a more productive and balanced state that will allow them to progress. Beech and Brockbank (1999), in their study of a mentoring scheme for thirty five junior and middle hospital managers, connected the dynamics of mentoring with Berne's (1977) work on ego states, and concluded that communication is only fully effective when it takes place between the positive aspects of those states. A general discussion of these concepts at the outset of the relationship can be helpful and even empower the mentee to mentor themselves, promoting self-reliance and resilience.

Applying these techniques can build empathic reinforcement in your mentee who feels truly understood and sympathised with. A mentee exposed to empathic reinforcement will quickly gain the confidence to creatively explore ideas and emotions in the mentoring conversation, encourage their own solutions and instil the self-assurance to test them.

Building rapport

All relationships begin with the process of rapport: either positive rapport leading to mutual understanding, or negative rapport risking complete discord. This may happen very quickly or develop over time but even an initial negative reaction in the dyad can be resolved and transformed into a workable relationship. Techniques exist which can aid and enhance this process and prove very useful in mentoring in creating trust and confidence, or in reassuring a shy or nervous mentee.

Rapport is the mechanism we use to build trust, credibility and empathy. People prefer others who are like themselves, and, through both verbal and non-verbal communication, it is possible to put your mentee at ease, identify with them and build a strong bond. Trust can make or break a mentoring relationship and the value of rapport cannot be overstated.

In order to establish rapport with your mentee it is first necessary to create rapport with yourself. Sometimes we are at odds with ourselves, for example, when trapped by indecision. Before engaging in the mentoring process it is important that you are in harmony with yourself and that any inner conflict is either resolved or under control to avoid it spilling out into the conversation.

Three considerations are pertinent to seeking rapport, either with your mentee or yourself:

1. *Setting*
   Thinking about the external factors and practicalities that may distract the mentoring encounter is a sensible place to start. Consider where you are meeting, whether it is comfortable, appropriate and safe. Maslow (1943) introduced the 'hierarchy of needs' theory: a list of requirements necessary to progress to the next level, serving to optimise the level of learning. So, for example, if the aim is to teach someone a different language, you should first look at the environment in which they will learn. Is it appropriate – a classroom not a pub, is it comfortable, are there chairs, light and heat, is it safe – are you in a war-zone? It might seem obvious but if you were trying to learn how to use a computer you would not get very far if there was no electricity supply available.

2. *Identity*
   Self-efficacy, understanding the limits of your own competence, is important in mentoring. Uncertainty quickly conveys itself to your mentee who could lose confidence in you. While training, reading and research significantly contribute to ability, the display of confidence (even if not completely feeling confident) has a conspicuous impact on the mentee. Behaving as the mentor you wish to be creates a positive cycle; self-assurance encourages your mentee to regard you with confidence reassuring you that you are the mentor you want to be and the cycle of reinforcement continues – each bolstering the other, both believing that the relationship is beneficial. Behave as a mentor, embrace that identity and others will soon regard you in the same way.

3. *Ethos*
Belief in the process and its value is possibly the most significant consideration, acting as the driver to the external and internal factors. Exploring your motivation to mentor can help develop a sound ethos. If you are mentoring for purely self-seeking gain, it may come across in the way you mentor. Most mentors are drawn to the activity for altruistic reasons and are usually unpaid for their efforts. They are ethos-driven and it shows, delivering that confidence and assurance to the mentee in the process. It should also be kept firmly in mind that mentee motivation is equally important; did they come of their own volition or did their manager send them? Being instructed to attend does not signify a doomed dyad but it is worth discussing and exploring this together to expose more positive motivations.

Having established a suitable environment, considered your own self-efficacy and confirmed your ethos let us now explore some simple rapport-building techniques.

When your mentee enters the room you should give immediate thought to how you intend to communicate both verbally and non-verbally. Verbal communication includes words, tone and timbre and all can be used to build rapport. Opening small talk is helpful in establishing the climate of trust and confidence needed to explore ideas, opinions, beliefs and values. Initial enquiry into their health, journey or, perhaps, finding a shared interest or hobby can ease those initial moments. Think about your tone and timbre; how you say words can impact on how they are received. A friendly, conversational tone can set the pace for the session. It is also helpful to paraphrase your mentee by summarising salient points and using the mentee's own words can promote empathy.

In human interaction more than half of overall communication consists of body language. It is possible to influence rapport from the outset without saying a word. Body language speaks volumes. To reinforce a welcome and inviting environment for your session, relax your shoulders and open up your posture; crossed arms and legs can be perceived as defensive. Consider your facial expressions, remember to smile and show when you are listening and that you are interested in what your mentee is saying. Eye contact is important to form a connection, but use relaxed vision and be aware that a stare of more than three seconds can be uncomfortable – blink! Using gestures to animate your words can also indicate interest. Think about your proximity to the mentee; too far could hinder rapport and too close may cause discomfort. Recognising that your body subconsciously informs others of the way you feel presents a timely reminder to avoid being judgemental. It is hard to hide.

The adoption of mirroring or matching techniques is useful for putting your mentee at ease. This is not mimicry and should be used judiciously. It is more an attempt to subtly duplicate the energy of your mentee through the replication of, for example, stance. So if your mentee leans forward to speak, lean in towards them slightly. Or, if they cross their right leg, cross your left ankle. This represents a clear, non-verbal signal of rapport, showing that you are on the same wavelength and that you can be trusted to listen, respect and understand them. Matching or mirroring your mentee is effective, but it should be used discreetly or your well-intentioned matching maybe mistaken for impersonation or parody.

Rapport can also be strengthened through discovering how the mentee learns and the way they communicate, variable features of every individual. Knowledge of learning styles can be utilised to enhance the mentoring process and to help the mentee's self-awareness and self-knowledge. There are many different categorisations of learning styles that can be quickly applied to help superficially build rapport. It is worth noting that Learning Styles have their critics. Coffield, Moseley, Hall and Eccleston (2004) question their effectiveness in light of the confusing range in existence. Nevertheless, we all learn and communicate in different ways and some knowledge of how this works provides a better appreciation of what makes people tick, a particularly useful intelligence for any mentor.

One such system, VAK (Visual, Auditory and Kinaesthetic) signals three representations of how an individual communicates. Equipped with this knowledge, the mentor is enabled to adopt appropriately focused language and paraphrasing to correspond with that communication style. This accord will be recognised and responded to. It also clearly demonstrates that you are listening.

A visual communicator uses descriptive words, such as 'I see', and if asked to describe a glass of water would focus on its appearance. An auditory communicator is influenced more by sound and uses terms like, 'I hear what you're saying'. A kinaesthetic communicator focuses on feelings so may comment, 'I understand'. Visual communicators are typically high energy, speak quickly and gesticulate to illustrate their meaning whereas kinaesthetic communicators have a more considered response, take their time and are more reflective. High-energy individuals may become frustrated with more ponderous low-energy people. Once the type of communicator is identified, it is relatively simple to match the energy displayed and to promote effective communication. Understanding how we communicate so that the response or behaviour can be better anticipated removes the frustration and impatience that can hinder an exchange.

A further example of learning styles is the popular Honey and Mumford model (1982). This categorises learners through four preferences. Firstly, Activist learners who approach new experiences with enthusiasm and an open mind with little reserve or caution. They thrive at managing immediate, crisis-laden problems through brainstorming and reactive thinking. Conversely, the Reflector learner adopts a more considered approach, observing and considering all perspectives before committing. The Reflector may be happiest researching, investigating and assembling information without feeling rushed or under pressure to make a decision. The Pragmatist learner likes to test theories or techniques and is particularly inventive: they excel at generating functional solutions. Finally, the Theorist learner is analytical, objective and logical, adept at understanding complexity. Some individuals fall into more than one or, even, all categorisations and the characteristics displayed may change over time or through personal development under the influence of the work role.

While certainly not prescriptive, learning styles can be useful in mentoring to help the mentee understand both themselves and others. Table 1 exemplifies the manner of question and mentoring approach best suited to each of these learning styles.

Table 1: HOW TO MENTOR USING LEARNING STYLES

How to mentor	Approach	Good question
An Activist	Involve them. For example, try role play, keep the session varied	Can you think of five ideas to solve this issue? Be as creative and outrageous as you like
A Reflector	Split discussions over two sessions to allow them time to consider before progressing	Would you like to think about our discussion quietly for five minutes within the session?
A Pragmatist	Invite them to choose a role model at work who possesses a trait or skill they admire and whom they can emulate	What coaching or mentoring model or technique from this selection would you like to apply to this discussion?
A Theorist	Suggest they brainstorm as many theories as they can find to address a specific area of concern or development	Are you making any underlying assumptions about this situation?

Learning styles can offer the basis for reflection on communicating with others, promoting self-awareness and enhancing emotional intelligence for both mentee and mentor.

Empathic listening

The most important skill applicable to all forms of mentoring is deep listening. Many people think they know how to listen but deep listening is rarely understood or practised. Yet it can provide the mentor with a most productive and effective tool serving not only the mentoring relationship but as a valuable, transferable skill which can enhance all aspects of our professional and personal relationships.

Listening may appear to be an inherently uncomplicated action but it actually functions at several levels:

- *Inactive:* total disengagement, where even if the word is heard, what is said is not.

- *Implied:* where listening is indicated but not fully captured. For example, a preoccupied dad absorbed in his newspaper as his child describes an eventful sports day while occasionally adding an implicit, carefully timed 'I see.'

- *Factual:* the basic form of listening where the facts are established but nothing deeper, such as underlying feelings. For example, the mentee says she/he is happy but is frowning. There is some level of disengagement.

- *Projective:* a good example of projective listening is where two politicians are seemingly engaged in a conversation but are in fact talking at each other rather than conversing; there is no exchange, each merely intent on voicing their own opinion.

- *Misinterpreted:* where a party to an interaction leaves with a completely different view from the other. It occurs more frequently than you would expect and is usually the result of a wish for something to happen being projected onto others.

- *Critical:* Where the listener, perhaps a lawyer, evaluates what is being said to identify weaknesses which they can then use to strengthen their own argument.

- *Active:* Active listening delivers a clear indication that you are listening. This can be reinforced through body language such as nodding and smiling or by verbal tools such as paraphrasing.

- *Empathic and mindful:* This is the level most suited to mentoring. It is a conscious, aware and reflective skill taking in the facts and demonstrating that you understand, you sympathise and you feel concern. It requires a great deal of practise and consideration.

We all need to be heard and feel we are understood; it is a basic human requirement. Applying empathic listening techniques to mentoring encounters can transform the relationship. Interestingly, if a mentor is an empathic listener and says little, the mentee can still leave with the impression of wisdom and knowledge, such is the power of listening.

We hear with our ears but we listen with our minds. When listening, the mind should be emptied of distractions and be fully present for your mentee. Pay attention not only to your mentee's words but their body language, facial expressions and gestures. Listen for the words unspoken and what any gaps may mean. Maintain relaxed eye contact, be non-judgemental regarding what you hear and use techniques such as paraphrasing to confer empathic reinforcement.

Begin by gathering the facts, use active listening techniques, such as nodding and eye contact, and be open to the mentee and what they have to say to achieve empathic listening. Apply the three degrees of listening (Figure 1) to encourage a powerful encounter. Sometimes, a good listener, acting as a sounding board, is all the mentee needs.

It is worth noting that mindful and empathic listening absorbs much concentration and energy which is why most mentoring conversations have a duration of approximately an hour. Even a short session where the mentee feels listened to and understood can be transformational.

Periodically remind yourself that to effectively listen you cannot talk. Most mentors find this discipline the hardest and yet it can be the most rewarding. When listening to an issue that you identify with it can be very tempting to jump in with an opinion or solution, but this is your solution, and by diverting the mentee's attention you risk missing their thoughts, ideas and approaches. Holding back allows the mentee to explore and verbalise their own thoughts and you may, in fact, learn something if it develops into a solution you had not considered. More crucially, it displays that you are interested in what they have to say and their ideas, allowing them to be creative and increasing their confidence – a key goal of mentoring. This requires practise, but the great news is it

Figure 1: THE THREE DEGREES OF DEEP LISTENING

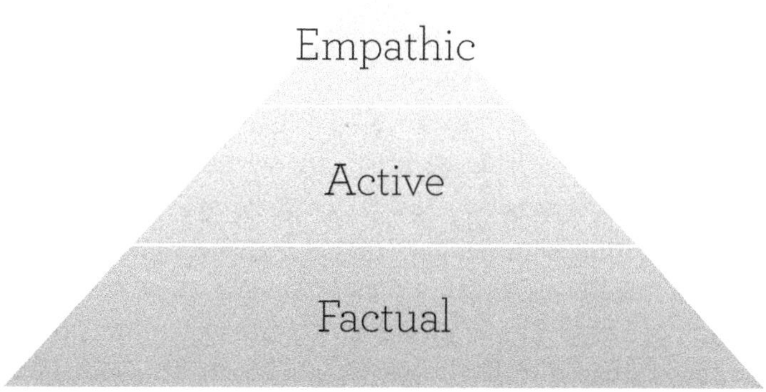

Empathic

Active

Factual

can be rehearsed in any situation with anyone. Try it at home with a family member, in a social situation or a casual work conversation. You will be surprised not only at what you can learn but also the regard in which you are held by the speaker. It also strengthens your ability to avoid the pitfall of politician's projective listening. Your mentee may well have chosen you for your expertise and guidance but it should still be very much a partnership. When a role model, a respected mentor, listens to you patiently, allows you to explore your ideas and shows interest and respect it is surprisingly empowering.

Patience lies at the heart of empathic listening, requiring the listener to not only gather the facts and show that they are listening but make the mentee feel understood and respected. This confirms their own validity and increases self-efficacy.

Powerful inquiry

Sitting alongside empathic listening is another of the key mentoring skills – powerful inquiry. Asking the right question puts the mentee in the 'starring role' and the centre of focus. It confirms that the process is participatory and that the mentee is a vital, legitimate partner. It also confers respect, recognising that while the mentor may be the authority on the profession, skill or organisation, the mentee is the expert on themselves. Acknowledging the importance of the contribution made by the self-expert boosts confidence and encourages the mentee to take responsibility in any resulting action. Furthermore, while the mentee may act upon the mentor's advice, if they have formulated their own solution (guided by the mentor through the use of judiciously timed and phrased questions) they are more likely to assume ownership and take action.

A powerful question can also help breach a seemingly insurmountable wall. Helping the mentee to consider an issue from a different angle or with a lesser emphasis can liberate the creative thought processes to find a solution.

In mentoring, some questions prove more constructive than others. For example, a closed question – one that requires a yes/no answer – may not be the best way to get your mentee talking. Helpful questions can challenge the mentee but, more significantly, can also shift perspectives; apparently insurmountable issues can be seen in new ways that lead to alternative resolutions. Such questions can be influential in guiding the mentee to achieve that 'light-bulb' moment: the point where they unveil a solution. Frustratingly, the mentor often fails to witness this revelatory moment as it usually occurs during a period of reflection. When it does happen within the session it is a very satisfying experience for both partners.

While the closed question is generally regarded as unhelpful it may be appropriate when there is simply a need to establish a fact. Some questions may be too challenging particularly the asking of 'why?' The impression of challenge could, however, be softened by the tone of voice adopted; if in doubt, 'what' should be used instead. Multiple questions, where several are asked at once (and often in the same breath), can also cloud the thought process. To avoid this, think before asking then pause for a response before moving on to the next. To combat a fear of forgetting a question it is better to write it down rather than expect your mentee to possess total recall. Another example of unhelpful questioning is when it is, in fact, advice masquerading as a question. This would begin with 'Don't you think', 'Couldn't you' or 'Shouldn't you', and then followed by a piece of advice. While such guidance can be very helpful it should not be phrased as a question when it clearly is not. Similarly, leading questions, pointing the mentee in the direction you think they should go, may occasionally be appropriate but risks closing the conversation to creative avenues other than your own.

A final aspect of unsympathetic questioning is more of a behavioural issue – interruption by talking over your mentee or finishing their sentences. This is deeply unhelpful. It denies the mentee the space to reflect and explore their own thoughts, and, when they do get a chance to speak, they feel pressurised to fill the space as quickly as possible before the opportunity disappears. This is an unexceptional issue for mentors, particularly where they have been sought out for their expertise, advice and guidance and so expect to be listened to, but it sets a poor communication example, shows little respect and can even undermine the mentee.

Table 2 shows how unhelpful questions can be readily converted by the addition of a few words or by slightly rephrasing the question:

Table 2:   EXAMPLES OF UNHELPFUL QUESTIONS

Type of question	Example	Rephrase question
Closed	Do you have time to take on that project?	How would your workload change if you take that on?
Challenging	Why did you refuse that promotion?	What reasons led you to this decision?
Leading	How did you feel: angry?	How did you feel: angry, relieved?

Powerful questions tend to be open and encourage the mentee to talk. Probing questions can help the mentee think more deeply about the issue or even adjust perspectives sufficiently to uncover a solution or idea. Examples of probing questions can involve examining the past: 'what led to this'?' This encourages the mentee to tell their story, at which point the mentor would act simply as a sounding board using empathic listening skills and open questions. Similar questions could be, 'have you experienced this before? What was the outcome? What would you do differently?' All these examples promote reflection on previous experience which leads to learning. It can also prove beneficial to look ahead: 'what would be the best possible outcome?', for example. This allows the mentee to review their goal, then work back in stages to determine how they could reach it. Reflecting on significance may also prove worthwhile: 'why is this significant for you? On a scale of one to ten, how important is it?' We often exaggerate problems to the point where they can become overwhelming. Analysing their significance carefully may draw out a realisation that they are not insurmountable.

Exploring feelings can reveal much about a mentee; 'how do you feel?' allows them to fully consider themselves and the impact of the issue faced. Even more powerful is, 'how do you think they feel?' which challenges the mentee to be empathic and consider the issue from another's point of view. This strategy is particularly helpful in dysfunctional relationships to rebuild understanding between parties.

An effective probing question is, 'who else could help you?' When under pressure we often feel isolated and a gentle reminder that others may be available to support and help can immediately relieve the pressure from the belief that responsibility for solving the issue is all yours.

Finally, demonstrating your observation is very powerful. 'You mentioned this earlier, tell me more' highlights both empathy and understanding as well as showing that you truly listened.

Powerful inquiry not only encourages and facilitates creative thought but also helps the dyad to negotiate any block in thinking or a seemingly insurmountable problem. Open or probing questions can be effective in dismantling the block or revealing a path to circumnavigate it. Other approaches include the five option technique, a coaching tool that requires the mentee to find five separate solutions to their problem. The solutions can be as outlandish and creative as the mentee's imagination can unearth. This is a fun tool which lessens the gravity of the issue in the mentee's mind and has no rules or boundaries limiting the options. At least one or two viable options usually surface from the mayhem and may be worthy of further investigation.

A frequent concern for inexperienced mentors is pinpointing the perfect question, which can cause them to stop listening to their mentee as they work out what to ask. It is far more preferable to pay heed to what is said and use reflection to identify powerful questions. Allowing half an hour following a mentoring session to consider the questions you asked and whether they could have been more helpful, raises your awareness. Anything missed can always be noted down and revisited at a later session. With experience, they are more likely to present themselves at the appropriate moment.

Should a specific powerful question not come to mind it is best to just remember that the most powerful questions are open ones, encouraging your mentee to talk and think freely. A far more powerful skill is empathic listening along with paraphrasing and using the mentee's own words. So if you are stuck try, 'tell me more.'

Compassionate challenge

One of the most effective yet potentially uncomfortable mentoring moments is where the mentor challenges the mentee, creating possible tension by placing the onus to resolve it on the mentee. When delivered with compassion and the mentee's best interests at heart, this 'critical friend' approach can strengthen belief in competency, self-reliance and the power of the mentee as they find their ability to settle issues for themselves. While the mentee may offer resistance by, for example, distraction or prevarication, it is important to sensitively bring them back to the core issue.

Scenario: a challenging conversation between David and Rosie

> *David:* In our last session we discussed strategies for you to approach your manager, Amy, and ask for a pay rise to recognise the additional responsibilities thrust upon you in the last couple of months. You favoured a direct approach by requesting a meeting with your manager; how did that go?
> *Rosie:* Well, to be honest with you, I just haven't had a chance.
> *David:* This was quite an issue for you in our last session; you were quite angry about it.
> *Rosie:* I still am, it's completely unfair and I've just found out that my colleague, Jack, is earning more than me for doing the same job as far as I can see.
> *David:* So you have a strong additional argument there to take to Amy.
> *Rosie:* Well, yes, I suppose so.
> *David:* You seem reluctant.
> *Rosie:* I'm just so busy, it's hard to find the time.

Rosie's reluctance to talk about her proposed meeting with Amy indicates a resistance that may lay at the heart of the matter and David slightly changes tactic by focusing on the possible cause of her discomfort despite Rosie clearly wishing to avoid it.

> *David:* How do you get on with Amy?
> *Rosie:* Good, yes, fine, we're fine.
> *David:* Tell me about your relationship.
> *Rosie:* It's good, fine, yes, you know she's a strong manager, a strong leader, very decisive, she knows what she wants. Once she's made a decision, nothing deters her – she's very strong. Not a great listener, if I'm honest. She's great you know, but not someone I'd feel comfortable talking to, you know. She's rather intimidating.

Rosie's anxiety is becoming clearer and David can now refocus on strategies to help Rosie approach Amy with greater confidence.

Reflection: the reluctance to engage may point to an issue requiring attention which a mentor should tactfully probe and challenge, although the mentor should acknowledge this will only succeed when the mentee is ready to talk. If the challenge is consistently sidestepped it may be more prudent to 'park it' and revisit at a later time. In Rosie's case if her resistance continued David could then have addressed any potential issues associated with Rosie's own confidence before returning to her interaction with Amy. Should it be unclear whether your mentee is ready for challenge, remember to seek out the verbal and non-verbal clues displayed but if doubt remains be cautious and defer. The main tenet for every mentor is ethical; do no harm.

Constructive feedback

There are many aspects of life where we are expected to give and receive feedback, yet we are rarely taught how to do so effectively. This represents a missed opportunity, not only to improve ourselves but to fashion an open, blame-free, creative environment where the prospect of higher productivity and a happier, more balanced workforce could exist.

Providing and receiving feedback can be awkward. Everyone enjoys positive feedback but it does not necessarily improve performance because we are naturally internally driven to do the best we can. Many also argue that negative feedback has little effect and can even make performance worse. Certainly, poorly delivered feedback is unlikely to boost either development or awareness.

Constructive feedback is only fully effective when the participants act in cooperation. It is important therefore to understand what makes each other tick so may not be advisable until the mentoring relationship matures. Feedback should be delivered with the best intentions and received with an open and learning mind, opening windows onto a world of new perspectives, transforming communication and improving understanding of ourselves, our colleagues and our clients.

It is vital to avoid damaging positive self-image. Receiving feedback that conflicts with that image can lead to cognitive dissonance – an imbalance in our world. It becomes easier and more comfortable for a recipient to discount such feedback or rationalise it in line with their self-image. This response represents a defence mechanism, a naturally human reaction to protect ourselves from perceived attacks. If, for example, your manager tells you that you are not meeting expectations, you may rationalise that by thinking that nobody could meet such high expectations.

Inviting the receiver of feedback to play a more equal role can provide the reassurance that the process does not merely focus on blame. An effective technique is to ask the receiver for their own impressions and invite them to critique themselves. Most people are aware of what can be improved and developed or what went well. Allowing them to lead the discussion, asking open questions and using their own words to guide them is enough to ensure a productive evaluative interchange that protects their self-image and avoids cognitive dissonance.

Being too diplomatic, however, is not always appropriate, particularly where an individual already has low self-awareness and knowledge. There are a number of tools designed to explore and strengthen self-awareness, a good example being Johari's Window (Luft and Ingham, 1955) which spotlights different aspects in self-knowledge. This model suggests that self-knowledge and awareness can be increased through self-disclosure and feedback leading to the emergence of potential.

Constructive feedback is a skill that could and should be conducted within the safe environment of a mentoring relationship where the dyad feels respected and valued. Agreement to give and receive constructive feedback and act as a critical friend to each other should be clarified at the opening session and each time the opportunity for feedback arises. This is an invaluable skill that reinforces resilience for both mentee and mentor.

Mindful reflection

Reflection is an essential element of mentoring, which is both enhanced and developed as a result. Reflection should be proactively encouraged by the dyad both individually and as a team within the mentoring session. It is how we learn and progress, enabling us to avoid repeating the same unhelpful behaviours. The essence and nature of powerful inquiry ensures that the mentee can critically reflect upon and analyse their experiences, ideas, feelings and thoughts. To do this mindfully and proactively, making it a key component of the mentoring relationship, allows it to become a positive process to aid learning, understanding and development.

A simple, helpful tool for both mentee and mentor is the maintenance of a reflective mentoring journal, a written record of your impressions, thoughts and feelings on the session and kept entirely confidential and purely for your own use. The mentee could also use the journal to record goals set and actions agreed, followed by a critically reflective account after the action: what went well, what could have been done differently. This can then form the basis for discussion in later sessions. The mentor can utilise the journal to reflect on learner type and learning style determined, or mentoring skills applied as a review of their own development. This could include details of any helpful listening skills adopted, the type of powerful questions asked and the effect they had, any unhelpful behaviours they could avoid, or what and how they could improve. For a more structured approach, exercises such as the Stem Reflection Triggers (Zachary, 2012: 3.2), where you apply a reflection model that can prompt powerful questions such as, 'what is working well, what is challenging?' to aid the process. Reflection transforms every mentoring encounter into a useful learning experience from which both mentor and mentee will grow.

Finding the time to reflect should be a deliberate, conscious action. It is important to plan moments of reflection before and after a session, booking reflection time in diaries. Allowing a few minutes to prepare to mentor or be mentored, then reflecting on what the session delivered and what may be considered at the next session is time well spent. This planned reflection may need to be supported by spontaneous reflection as a result of an issue arising during the course of a mentoring conversation. Pausing to reflect on what has been said or what something might mean can be very helpful in directing a conversation, but it should be used judiciously to avoid awkward interruptions or generally disturbing the flow of the session. The use of these reflective pauses should be agreed during preliminary mentoring sessions. If the issue is one that causes a block in either mentor or mentee, it is another instance where it could be parked for a later session after due reflection.

Summary

Regardless of who or why you are mentoring, some universal skills, shown in Figure 2, need to be honed to be effective. Being truly empathic by suspending judgement and minimising bias is the first discipline to master. This can then be communicated to the mentee through rapport building. The mentor can continue to support their mentee through inquiry, challenge, feedback and reflection, but the most important and powerful mentoring skill is the ability to listen and ensure the mentee feels listened to. Of all the skills this is the one that requires constant practise and vigilance regardless of experience, knowledge or expertise. It is also one of the most effective transferable skills with the potential to transform not only working relationships but all relationships and mould you into a more considerate, thoughtful and effective communicator.

Figure 2:   MENTORING SKILLS BUILDING BLOCKS

CHAPTER TIPS

Before deciding upon the skills you need to adopt to best help your mentee, you should first consider what sort of mentor they need. The mentor persona can take many forms:

- the Encourager: who will make you wonder what you can achieve
- the Role Model: whose behaviours you will try to emulate
- the Empowerer: who can restore self-confidence
- the Inspirer: who can make you braver

What type of influential mentor will you be?

CHAPTER 3
Mentoring Models

Before launching headlong into any formalised mentoring arrangement, it is first advisable to allocate some time to consider which approach is most appropriate to achieve the intended outcomes. Essentially, there are two predominant categories: traditional or sponsorship, also referred to as the American model which has a career development focus (Ensher, Thomas and Murphy, 2001), and developmental, also known as the European model, with a psychosocial function aimed at strengthening and underpinning interpersonal skills (Connor and Pokora, 2007).

Traditional mentoring

Founded in North America, this is the most familiar and identifiable of mentoring models. Traditional mentoring typically consists of an experienced, knowledgeable mentor who possesses a set of skills, or a position or role to which their mentee aspires. The mentor utilises this expertise to advise, guide and steer the mentee to, for example, a stronger organisational position. The mentor may also act as a kind of sponsor, facilitating introductions to people in positions of power, or to serve as an advocate or champion to promote the mentee's cause. The mentor may guide the mentee on organisational politics, advancement strategies and business etiquette or skills specific to the mentee's field.

The traditional mentoring model operates under the following four stages (Kram, 1985) which provide its structure and charts the transition through the relationship:

1. The relationship begins with 'initiation' where the relationship itself is established. It represents the 'getting to know you' stage and provides the foundation to clarify and align expectations of both mentor and mentee and the overall objective. If not clearly understood by the dyad it can lead to a misalignment of expectations.
2. The core mentoring function can then be launched in the stage that Kram calls 'cultivation'. This is where the relationship matures, specific goals are defined and strategies developed to achieve these aims.
3. Kram's third stage is 'separation' where the outcomes of the relationship are assessed and its conclusion effectively planned and managed.
4. 'Redefinition' is the final step in the process, where the dyad determines either to part or re-establish a new mentoring relationship to tackle fresh issues.

The tone of the traditional model is one of 'telling'. The mentor guides, advises and leads the mentee to their identified goal. The initiation stage determines the framework for establishing a relationship with clear parameters that both mentor and mentee find comfortable, then, through deliberation, the mentee's objective is identified both for the individual session and the overall relationship. Essentially, it is where the ground rules are discussed and agreed and the purpose of the engagement clarified.

The mentoring process really begins at the cultivation stage. It usually opens with the mentee describing their 'story', the background of why they are there and what they want to achieve. While this may have been alluded to during initiation, it is explored in detail during cultivation. This is a vital component in the drive for a successful outcome as it allows the mentor to acquire a full understanding of the mentee's goal and motivations. The mentor employs their experience and expertise to guide the mentee to carry this through, helping them set smaller targets as part of their overall goal, plan out strategies using techniques such as role play and provide support through both disappointments and successes.

The following scenarios illustrate a typical dialogue between a mentor and mentee in a 'traditional model' at early and late stage cultivation:

Scenario: supporting disappointment: a traditional mentoring conversation between George (mentor) and Siân (mentee)

Siân has just begun her mentoring relationship with George. They have had their first few meetings and established a rapport that both felt comfortable with. She had initially approached George to be her mentor because of his standing in the organisation which she felt could enhance her own position and help her achieve promotion.

George: Siân, in our first meeting we established our mentoring contract. Are you still OK with this?

Siân: Absolutely.

George: In the following meeting we established that you would like to raise your profile in the company as you are ambitious, and would like to plan your career progression. The meeting after that, our last meeting, we first discussed ways of achieving this and came up with a strategy. You were going to put yourself forward to sit on the Policies and Procedures Committee after I identified an opening.
How did that go?

Siân: Not very well, I'm afraid.

George: What happened?

Siân: I approached the Chair, Rosie, to express my interest but I got a rather lukewarm reception. In fact, she was rather blunt. She felt I lack experience, which I suppose is true. I feel a bit despondent about the whole thing to be honest.

George: Rosie is under pressure at the moment but it's a shame she won't give you a chance. However, she is losing Megan from the Committee and she brought a great deal of experience with her so that is quite a loss. Let's change tack and think about the experience you do have. I know that next month there will be an opening on the Staff Development Committee, you've got experience in that haven't you?

Siân: Yes, a great deal. I've worked in human resources and in training previously; actually I contributed to a number of strategies in those posts.

George: Excellent, I'll introduce you to the Chair, Dee. You can mention your interest and ensure you talk about all the experience you can bring. Be direct and straight to the point, Dee doesn't appreciate flattery or waffle.

Reflection: George helps Siân to understand Rosie's rejection and offers an alternative option, using his knowledge and experience to advise on Siân's approach. George, in these early stages, is clearly in control of the mentoring process.

The power balance at the beginning of the relationship sits clearly with the mentor while the mentee assumes a passive, learning role. Over time there should be a shift to a more equal footing, for as the mentee learns and develops, their confidence will grow. Selecting the optimum moment to relinquish power rests on the mentor's skill and discretion; too much independence too soon may result in errors of judgement or want of guidance. Too little independence can suppress development and inhibit progress by dulling enthusiasm and ambition. Managing the power shift often causes anxiety in mentors; judging the perfect moment to hold back advice and let the mentee take control can be difficult and is often achieved through a process of trial and error. Any miscalculation can soon be identified and easily rectified as in the following case of George and Siân. Failures should be regarded more as learning opportunities.

Scenario: a power shift between George (mentor) and Siân (mentee)

Siân has now been mentored by George for the past three months, developing ways to raise her profile within the organisation with a view to eventual promotion. These strategies have proved effective and Siân has increased her organisational presence through participation in committees that has heightened her reputation.

> *George:* Siân, I think this would be a timely point to review our strategy. Your reputation is quite strong now so we should talk about approaching your manager.
> *Siân:* I agree; it feels like the right time. I've got a meeting with Sophie tomorrow and I'm going to broach the subject with her.
> *George:* Be direct with her, you are in a strong position at the moment, so just demand the promotion.
> *Siân:* I don't think that would work with Sophie; in the past she has responded to me more positively if I take a more passive role.
> *George:* That's not been my experience, I've always been direct and straight with her which she seems to appreciate.
> *Siân:* I think that may be more to do with your position in the company.
> *George:* Fair point. Ok, how will you approach it?
> *Siân:* A little less directly. I'll point out the benefits of promoting me into position: that my experience as a supervisor and knowledge and reputation will enhance the department. I'll also suggest Matt as my replacement. Sophie will want solutions and he has stood in for me a few times; it would be an easy transition. I think if she can see the benefits and what I could bring to the role first, before I ask outright, she'll be more inclined to agree.
> *George:* That sounds great and remind her of your activities outside the department too.
> *Siân:* I will, thanks George.

Reflection: George has wisely recognised Siân's wish for independence and supported it. While he may not agree with her approach, he realises that Sophie may be influenced by his position and respond to him differently. Equally, Siân could be wrong but he acknowledges the need for a power shift. If the strategy fails, he will re-evaluate the options but first ensure that Siân's confidence is undamaged by the attempt. It represents a crossroad in the relationship and the mentee will need to be reassured whatever the outcome. A discussion about power shifts may help the mentee to realise that they are beginning to take control and that the risk of failure is part of that experience.

Exercising power or control over a relationship also comes with much responsibility. The mentee, in particular, is vulnerable to manipulation, either deliberate or unintentional. Mentors have been known to exploit mentee ideas for their own benefit, and negative behaviours such as this can be labelled 'toxic', a subject fully explored later in this book.

The final stages of separation and redefinition may appear to be less important, yet when neglected can lead to a number of issues and even toxicity. A mentoring relationship can be intense and significant for both parties. Neglecting to finish it appropriately, through mutual feedback, next step discussions and, crucially, the celebration of the interaction, can lead to feelings of loss and regret in either or both parties. It would be a shame to end a positive intervention on a sour note. A successful mentoring relationship should be looked back on with pride at accomplishment and gratitude to your mentoring partner. It is the responsibility of both to commit to an appropriate closure as, by the end of the process, they should feel on a more equal footing as the balance of power evens out.

Developmental mentoring

Developmental mentoring is closer in style to coaching than to traditional mentoring. The dyad work as a partnership to encourage discussion and address issues. The mentor recognises the value, knowledge and experience brought to the relationship by the mentee. The model implies that the mentee is the expert on themselves while the role of the mentor is to help them uncover answers through the use of techniques such as asking thought-provoking and powerful questions.

The origins of developmental mentoring arose when Kram (1985) analysed the detailed components of mentoring and isolated two discernible mentor functions:

- sponsorship, based on the mentor's senior position in an organisation
- psychosocial, which focuses on interpersonal/communication development.

Although traditional mentoring also features both functions it is predominately associated with sponsorship, whereas the developmental approach places emphasis on interpersonal development and it is more akin to peer mentoring type models where colleagues of an equal standing mentor each other to basically act as sounding boards for ideas and issues. The proportion of peer mentoring models in comparison to sponsorship mentoring is more evident where hierarchical organisational structures are reduced or non-existent (McManus and Russell, 2007). This, no doubt, explains the popularity and origins of traditional mentoring in North America, where mentoring flourishes in the corporate environment.

Allen, Eby, Poteet, Lentz and Lima (2004) describe the purpose of the psychosocial function as holding subjective outcomes, such as career satisfaction, and the sponsorship function as holding objective outcomes, such as promotion. Psychosocial mentoring is also positively related to resilience (Kao et al., 2014). Psychosocial functions are more dependent on the quality of the mentoring relationship and satisfaction with the mentor due to the intensity of the relationship. This highlights the difference in styles of the two models: traditional being more direct and developmental more indirect and consequently more time-consuming. The traditional mentor will tell the mentee what to do, the developmental mentor will prompt the mentee to create their own solutions.

The following scenario mirrors the previous example for traditional mentoring but with the dialogue reflecting a developmental model approach. Note the difference in emphasis.

Scenario: supporting disappointment: a developmental mentoring conversation between George (mentor) and Siân (mentee)

Siân has just begun her mentoring relationship with George; they have had their first few meetings and established a rapport that both feel comfortable with. She approached George to mentor her because of his standing in the organisation which she felt could enhance her own position and help her achieve promotion.

> *George:* Siân, in our first meeting we established our mentoring contract. To ensure this is still effective, let's take a moment to revisit it.

Siân and George spend time talking through the previous contract and conclude that they are both still happy with it.

> *George:* At the next meeting we established that you would like to raise your profile in the company as you are ambitious and would like to plan your career progression. The meeting after that, our last meeting, we began discussing ways of achieving this and you suggested a more visible role. I was aware of a forthcoming vacancy on the Policies and Procedures Committee which you were going to find out about. How did that go?
> *Siân:* Well, I discovered the Chair is Rosie and approached her to express my interest but I got a rather lukewarm reception. In fact, she was rather blunt. She felt I lack experience which I suppose is true. I feel a bit despondent about the whole thing to be honest.
> George – Take me through the conversation. How did you start?
> *Siân:* I don't really know her. I just approached her in the corridor and asked her straight out.
> [Siân pauses, George says nothing but listens and nods in an encouraging, non-judgemental way].

Siân: I suppose it may have been better to make an appointment, perhaps be more formal with my request.
George: How did Rosie respond?
Siân: She seemed harried and a little annoyed I think, perhaps rushed. On reflection I should have approached her more formally rather than spring it on her like that.
George: Rosie said you lacked experience, how do you feel about that?
Siân: I suppose that's true, but how can I get experience if I'm not given the chance to learn.
George: What experience do you have that you think might be useful.
Siân: My background is human resources with a bit of staff training, not policies and procedures directly but there is some of that in there, and I do think I could have contributed.
George: Are there any other committees or activities you could get involved in more that may increase your experience?
Siân: Well, actually they are looking to form a working group to draw up a skills matrix for the company, see what untapped talent is out there. I could get involved with that; I've done that sort of thing in the past.
George: That sounds very positive, I believe Megan is involved with that.
Siân: Yes, and Rosie is advising on it so there's a chance she could see me in a different light. Perhaps I'll drop Megan a line and let her know that I'm interested.

Reflection: George's help is less direct in this scenario but Siân still applies an understanding to Rosie's rejection which she can better accept and offers her own alternative. This approach represents a more equal interaction. George may also appreciate why Rosie rejected Siân but holds back, recognising that Siân's conclusion is just as valid. The crucial outcome is that Siân is no longer despondent and her confidence is restored.

The term 'developmental' is directed at the relationship rather than the individual, charting its progress over time. Hay's (1995: 3) 'developmental alliance' between mentor and client recognises the development of both parties and the more active role assigned to the mentee, compared to the more passive one of the traditional mentee. The developmental relationship meets the individual's development needs, and is also ascribed the term 'evolutionary'. Evolutionary mentoring, according to Brockbank and McGill (2006), recognises the mentee's social reality, and could be employed to tackle such situations as an oppressive or discriminatory environment that might inhibit learning. The mentor seeks to acquire an appreciation of the mentee's subjective world and uses this to help the mentee evolve into a position of personal power, aiding learning and development. Developmental mentoring also takes this broader, more holistic view.

Megginson et al. (2006) conceived the notion of a five-stage model of developmental mentoring based on Kram's earlier four-stage sponsorship model (1985) described previously. They argued that developmental mentoring required an additional stage at the beginning of the relationship reflecting its importance and split Kram's initiation stage into Rapport Building and Setting Direction:

- *Stage 1:* Rapport Building (initiation): the skills required to find and deliver a successful way of working together include establishing a contract in an open, non-judgemental and collaborative way.
- *Stage 2:* Setting Direction addresses goal-setting where diagnostic frameworks are used to pinpoint objectives and is combined with stage 3.
- *Stage 3:* Progression in Kram's Cultivation stage. The Progression stage involves challenging the mentee as well as recognising their achievements and is a highly active and productive period.
- The remaining two stages, Winding Up and Moving On, reflect Kram's original concept.

Later research undertaken on the model (Washington, 2013, 2016; Washington and Cox, 2016) resulted in a further refinement (distal mentoring) explored in chapter 6 of this book.

Comparisons and contrasts

Despite clear differences in the approach and focus of the two models, there are common internally and externally driven features in both ideology and application. The most salient of these are commitment, empathy, emotional dexterity and effective listening. The desire for self-enhancement and an altruistic intent to support the enhancement of others paradoxically go hand-in-hand in the mentoring sense, as the more able a mentor becomes, the abler they are to help their mentee. This commitment must come from within yet while the other factors are also preferably inherent, they are all capable of being learnt through training and experience.

The principle factor separating the more directive traditional model from its developmental confederate is best reflected in Ensher, Thomas and Murphy's (2001: 420) simplistic definition of it as 'a dyadic relationship in which the mentor, the senior person in age or experience, provides guidance and support to the less experienced person, the protégé.' The term 'protégé', as a reference to the 'mentee, originates from the North American traditional model of mentoring. The nature of the developmental mentoring model differs by aiming to help people 'take charge of their own development, to release their potential and to achieve the results that they value' (Connor and Pokora, 2007: 6). Rolfe (2012) provides a comparison between traditional and contemporary thinking, charting how mentoring has evolved, demonstrating its flexible nature.

The framework in Table 3 more readily clarifies the differences between the two approaches. The contrast is quite striking, but both have a role to play in mentoring in the workplace.

Table 3: DIFFERENCES BETWEEN TRADITIONAL AND DEVELOPMENTAL MENTORING

Traditional	Developmental
Intent: hierarchical Traditional schemes will often target specific groups identified by the organisation as worthy of development investment, for example, middle managers with leadership aspirations	*Intent:* inclusive Open to any employee interested in development
Skill: focused Mentors usually in influential senior positions with expert knowledge of mentee's area and the organisation	*Skill:* facilitative Mentors do not need to be expert in mentee/s area or organisational politics
Style: directive/telling Mentor provides the benefit of their wisdom, advice and guidance. They will provide the answer or solution	*Style:* enabling/asking Mentors are non-directional using skills such as powerful questions to guide the mentee, offering a new perspective, helping them to create their own solutions
Reason: professional development Useful for mentees seeking guidance specific to their profession or organisation	*Reason:* personal development Useful for mentees seeking personal development that will enhance their career

Which model to use

It is important for both mentor and mentee to understand the model to be adopted in the mentoring process, even if not by name, then at least in terms of intent. The choice depends on what the mentee wants to achieve, how the mentor intends to support them and the aspirations of the scheme sponsor.

If the organisation wishes to develop aspirant leaders to meet succession planning objectives, it may well opt for a traditional scheme, whereby promising employees are identified and paired with current leaders to guide them and impart their experience and expertise. Alternatively, a business may have a high absence record and use a developmental scheme to promote well-being in the workplace. There are also hybrid schemes that may start with a traditional intent then adapt to a developmental style, or be used for a mentee who wishes to not only advance their career but also enhance their personal development. Table 4 indicates how either model could be usefully applied to the same event. Provided they lead to organisational benefits or personal enrichment the choice of model is almost inconsequential. Unless there are positive outcomes the whole process becomes irrelevant.

Table 4: USE OF TRADITIONAL-TELL AND DEVELOPMENTAL-ASK MODELS

Scenario	Traditional-telling	Developmental-asking
1. Anna has overlooked me for promotion even though I am the most experienced in her team	Anna appreciates a direct approach; challenge her decision and remind her of the experience you would bring to the role	Can you think of the reasons why you were overlooked? How could you strengthen your position and ensure you are selected next time
2. The project I am sharing with Rosie is failing. She keeps taking over and bullying me into decisions I am not happy with but I cannot seem to stand up to her	Explain to her that you are equally responsible for the project. Agree a process for each decision whereby you both put your arguments forward before agreeing the best way forward	Why do you think Rosie is so assertive; does she feel under additional pressure? How could you feel more confident in articulating your point of view?
3. Oscar keeps stealing my ideas and presenting them as his own, he never mentions me	When you first share your ideas make sure it is in front of a group, not just Oscar and every time its mentioned make sure you are acknowledged	Is the idea a result of your discussion with Oscar; did he add anything to its development? Have you raised this with him? Is he aware of your feelings?
4. My colleague Ginny is worrying me; she keeps getting in late. I've covered for her but it's only a matter of time before we are both found out	Talk to her, explain the risks and that you cannot continue. Offer help. Encourage her to contact the Personnel department for support	Is she aware of what you are doing and the possible consequences for both of you? Does she need additional support? Is it simply poor timekeeping or is there a hidden reason?
5. All I want is promotion but I can't seem to get noticed by the senior management	You need to get involved in a project that will make you stand out. I can introduce you to an opportunity.	What strategies have you tried so far? How can they be improved? Is there another reason, for example, self-confidence?

In each of these scenarios, the traditional mentor offers direct advice and guidance to a solution based on their experience and knowledge. This is particularly effective if your mentor is familiar with the various organisational politics and knows the best strategies to secure the desired outcome. The model relies heavily on the mentor's expertise and ability to provide the right direction. The developmental mentor will ask questions to offer a fresh perspective to the mentee. They may feel they have a solution but will allow the mentee to first discover their own path before offering it. In doing so the mentor, coincidentally, often uncovers approaches new to them, enriching their own development, learning through their mentee. In the second scenario, for example, the traditional mentor offers straightforward advice to encourage the mentee to be more assertive with Rosie. The developmental mentor shifts the perspective, inviting the mentee to look at the issue from Rosie's point of view and to consider the possible causes of Rosie's behaviours. The advice of both mentors' may be based on additional knowledge of Rosie but while the traditional mentor would make full use of that knowledge, the developmental mentor would put it to one side to allow other avenues to open up. Determining the better approach for the mentee very much depends on their reaction to it. As a mentor, possessing all the available strategies, tools and techniques allows you to try different approaches with your mentee to identify which works best.

A more detailed review of applied mentoring is contained in chapter 5 Mentoring Schemes and many other aspects of developmental mentoring can be found in chapter 6 Distal Mentoring, which adapts the developmental mentoring format.

Summary

In this chapter we explored the two main models of mentoring; traditional and developmental, and considered their make-up, application and use. These two very different approaches have distinct intent and style but the most successful schemes often combine them to form a hybrid methodology, tailor-made for the organisation or individual. An adroit mentor will understand each approach and be able to utilise them as their mentee's needs require. In this respect, a mentor's versatility and adaptability is their most potent accomplishment.

CHAPTER TIPS

Mentoring is flexible, you may select a traditional approach if, for example, you need to meet regulatory or organisational directives. If, however, you require innovation or need to expand the pool of available mentors, then developmental may be more appropriate. Alternatively, you may apply developmental techniques to a traditional structure and create a hybrid model of mentoring; choose according to your needs.

CHAPTER 4
Toxic Mentoring

The intent of mentoring is to empower mentees to take charge of their own learning and development, and to achieve self-prescribed goals (Connor and Pokora, 2007: 6); at the same time, the mentor can develop skills and learning as well as enhance their own organisational standing. The relationship is intended to imbue both parties with a positive experience, stimulating mutual growth and development.

Emergent concepts of mentoring point to the utilisation of a mixture of approaches to cultivate positive mentoring, i.e. pushing and pulling styles (Hamlin and Sage, 2011), and to recognise the influence of psychosocial support (Kram, 1983). Even these positive approaches, however, can be inhibited by the presence of contrary factors within the relationship, potentially triggering a sense of personal failure and intensifying the harm exacted on either or both parties as a consequence.

What is toxicity?

While the term has only recently found its way into the mentoring vocabulary, evidence of relational impairment or failure, albeit sparse, has been apparent for much longer. Descriptions for toxic mentoring relationships include 'negative', 'dysfunctional' and 'ineffective'. Colourful phrases such as 'mentor from hell' or tormentor (Megginson and Clutterbuck, 2005: 25; Feldman, 1999) draw attention to such disagreeable characteristics as arrogance, over-familiarity or always talking and never listening. Toxicity can implant doubt in delicate relationships, question commitment and unbalance trust. Apart from the damage it may cause to an individual's self-belief and resilience, its insidious nature also threatens to sour wider professional relationships and even organisational morale.

Symptoms that can induce toxicity are diverse, ranging from the relatively mild where, for instance, a mentee consistently arrives late or cancels meetings, to a mentor who burdens the mentee with his/her own problems. There is also an assortment of causes covering mismatched expectations, scheduling difficulties and neglect of structural separation; where the mentor retires or changes job (Eby and Allan, 2002; Eby and Lockwood, 2005). It is reasonable therefore to label toxicity as the result of any behaviour that impairs the common intent of the mentoring process.

Toxicity from the perspective of the mentee

The consequences experienced from the actions of a toxic mentor can be hugely damaging, undermining confidence and adversely affecting future mentoring alliances or even other professional relationships. The psychological bond within a mentoring dyad is often intense, and breaches of trust or commitment can be perceived as a betrayal by a vulnerable mentee.

Toxic mentor behaviours can include:

- distracted behaviour, not fully paying attention
- poor listening skills causing the need to repeat, leading to misunderstanding
- neglectful inattention
- insufficient commitment
- lack of expertise/competence
- manipulative behaviours
- souring or transference whereby the mentor's disenchantment influences the mentee
- boundary violations
- professional violation, for example, misappropriation of the mentee's work or ideas
- contriving to use the mentee as unofficial labour

Whether confronted by a relatively minor infringement of the mentoring relationship, such as distraction, or a serious transgression of trust as in claiming the mentee's work for their own, it is impossible to accurately measure the effect toxicity has actually caused as feelings are so subjective. One person may take a setback in their stride while another with a more sensitive emotional response may regard the same incident as overwhelming.

A study of a UK public services mentoring scheme (Washington, 2016) found that while a low number of participants had experienced toxicity, the effects could be significant. In describing their experience, comments such as 'poisonous', 'doing more harm than good', and 'using the relationship for their own ends' are disturbing. One participant eloquently captured the chronic or long-term nature of toxicity describing it as 'nuclear waste ... seeping through the relationship . at the time ...and later on.' Another described how she measures toxicity, 'by the lasting effect it has . . . the toxic element would stay.'

The presence of a subtler form of toxicity often goes unrecognised by the dyad. An ineffective mentor may inflict significant damage through the use of poor skills, unwise advice or insipid manners, allowing harmful effects to creep in and undermine the mentee's confidence without them having any obvious appreciation of the root cause. This insidious connection is, arguably, more perilous than an openly hostile association as the mentee may unjustifiably assume responsibility for its failure.

Scenario: Rhys's brush with toxicity

> *Rita:* OK Rhys, last time we met I asked you to write up your ideas for this new product you designed.
> *Rhys:* That's right, I've produced a report. I was thinking of taking it to Rosie, maybe make a pitch to her.
> *Rita:* Well, why don't you pitch it to me first and we can see if it's worth going any further with it.
> *Rhys:* OK.

Rhys confidently takes Rita through a detailed plan for his product referring to his written report.

> *Rita:* I am sorry; Rosie won't go for this as it stands. Look, give me the report and I will try and refine a pitch for her.
> *Rhys:* Well, I appreciate your help with it but I would like to be there when you talk to her, present it with you.

Rita is vague but promises to keep Rhys in touch. When Rhys reminds her the following week Rita claims that the idea got nowhere. Three months later the product is launched. When questioned Rita maintains that the pitch had not worked but clearly Management had reconsidered.

Reflection: Was Rita's behaviour of deliberate intent or an honest mistake? While Rita's interest in the product is understandable, the mentoring conversation should have focused on how Rhys could make his pitch rather than what he was pitching. Rita's undue interest in the minutiae of the product and her vague response to a joint presentation to Rosie is a troubling sign. At that point, an email to Rita with an electronic copy of the report to help her make the initial pitch would have been more judicious while corroborating his ownership and her potential misappropriation. It might also give Rita pause for thought before succumbing to temptation.

Toxicity from the perspective of the mentor

Few studies exist that purely explore the mentor's experience of toxicity and yet its impact can be as devastating as it is for the mentee. The focus on the mentee stems from the popularity of the traditional mentoring model where the dynamics and control are weighted toward the mentor. The power equilibrium of the developmental model links the rise of mentors experiencing toxicity to the growing popularity of this model. While mentee reactions and feelings have long been explored, the mentor's viewpoint has been largely overlooked. Awareness is growing of the damage that can be inflicted by a toxic mentee (Eby and McManus, 2004; Allen, 2007; Eby, Butts, Durley, Ragins, 2010), although it remains an under-researched issue.

When a mentor experiences toxicity it has repercussions on motivation and confidence (Allen, 2007) where negative experiences can adversely affect the desire to mentor again. Differing relational needs between mentor and mentee (Eby and McManus, 2004) suggest that despite comparable experiences, there are significant variations in what each may find toxic.

Toxic mentee behaviours can include:

- submissiveness
- unwillingness to learn
- lack of engagement, commitment or being overly distracted
- manipulative behaviours
- boundary violations
- professional violation, for example, misappropriation of the mentor's work or ideas
- contriving to use the mentor as unofficial labour

Some of these behaviours are common to the toxic mentor list but where mentor toxicity tends to be more proactive, passive toxicity can be equally damaging, impinging on growth and nullifying the benefits.

Scenario: Megan and Jasper reach an impasse

> *Megan:* So Jasper, last time we discussed how you could assert yourself more in team meetings. You were going to review the agenda, decide what you were going to say and try it. How did that go?
> *Jasper:* I didn't get the chance.
> *Megan:* To see the agenda or speak?
> *Jasper:* Both. I didn't see the point in trying.
> *Megan:* Were there any items that you could have commented on or you had something to say about?
> *Jasper:* Not really.
> *Megan:* Surely the project you are supporting came up?
> *Jasper:* Yes, I worked really hard on that and I didn't get a mention, again.
> *Megan:* Could you have perhaps joined in the discussion at any point? Talked about your contribution.
> *Jasper:* I don't really see the point.

Reflection: Megan continues to suggest ways for Jasper to engage which he resists. This blocking behaviour may arise from a lack of confidence, a disengagement with the mentoring process, or an unresolved issue with the mentor. Maybe Jasper was obliged to undertake mentoring. His unwillingness is unlikely to be resolved through Megan's solutions. Possibly revisiting the mentoring contract would help to explore any undiscussed issues and give Megan the chance to secure commitment through reiterating the potential benefits for Jasper.

Some people seek mentoring with a clear idea of what they want to achieve and the mentor's job is that much easier. Others may be unsure or conflicted and may need more time to clarify their ideas through the mentoring process. The language they use may therefore appear confused, unclear, or they may display disengaged or unresponsive behaviours. The mentor's role here is to carefully listen and gently probe to find coherence in their thoughts and intentions. This may call for considerable patience in forming the driving force and rationale for the whole process. Making hasty assumptions can put you on the wrong path.

Unresolved toxicity can damage the mentor's sense of efficacy, eroding confidence and affecting behaviour which in turn increases the likelihood of further toxic encounters due to feelings of inadequacy as the mentor becomes trapped in an Anxiety Loop (see Figure 3).

Figure 3:   ANXIETY LOOP

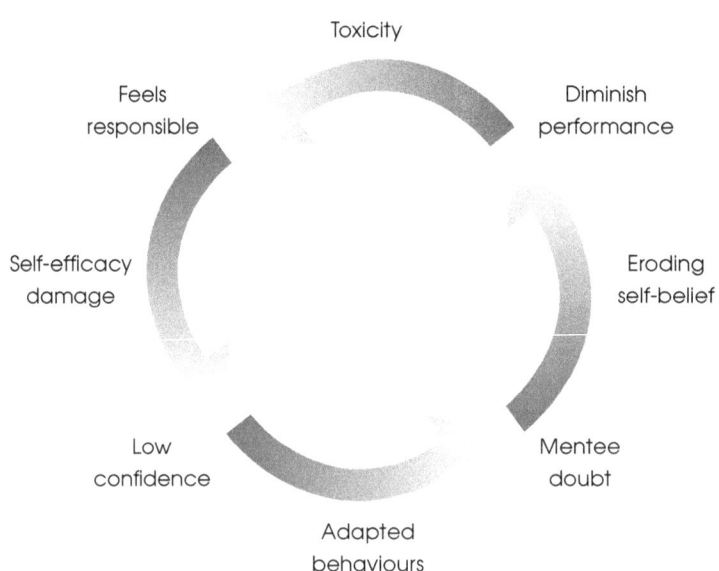

Any lack of mentor self-belief or conviction in their abilities or skills communicates itself non-verbally to the mentee, undermining faith in the mentor. The mentee's uncertainty then transfers to the mentor and a further erosion of morale. This low esteem inevitably influences the mentor's will to continue mentoring.

A common misconception among mentors is that any difficulty or breakdown in the relationship is due to their own shortcomings, which is both unhelpful and erosive. Toxicity can originate from mentor, mentee and the dyad in combination. It can be deliberate or unintentional, internal or external. The dyad may have been poorly matched or the result of inadequate understanding of the scheme or mentoring itself. Or it could be that as mere human beings we sometimes just don't get on. One may like to discuss detail, the other may prefer to look at the bigger picture. Ways can be found to effectively communicate but both parties need to be open and committed to it; if all else fails, it is perfectly acceptable to discontinue the relationship without guilt or feelings of failure.

As a mentor every effort should be made to also be a mentee. This represents an important form of supervision, an opportunity to see the mentoring relationship from a mentee viewpoint, augmenting experience and, of course, self-development. In committing to mentoring it is important to practise what you preach. Table 5 highlights some situations to watch out for that are precursors to toxicity.

Table 5 ARE YOU TOXIC?

Are you a toxic mentor?	Solution	Are you a toxic mentee?	Solution
Do you find you talk more than your mentee?	Encourage your mentee to talk, to tell their story. If you have a solution or idea, set it aside and see what they come up with first, it may surprise you	Do you discount your mentor's ideas or solutions?	Pause before you reject them, it may be that trying the solution will work or lead you to discover your own answer
Do you struggle to attend meetings because you are so busy?	Decide now whether you want to mentor and if you do prioritise the activity. Letting your mentee down merely underlines their lack of importance to you and it is rude	Do you boast to colleagues about your mentor?	The mentoring contract is a confidential one which protects what you say, allowing you the freedom to explore issues creatively. It is also there to protect your mentor. Respect the process and your mentor and instead of boasting why not encourage colleagues to seek a mentor too?
Your mentee is brilliant; you are afraid they will eclipse you	Remember why you are mentoring: to help your mentee grow and develop. Their success will inevitably reflect well on you – enjoy it	Your mentor wants you to contribute ideas, but you are afraid to	Mentoring will increase your confidence if you trust your mentor. You are in a safe environment; any idea is worthy of consideration. This is the arena to try it out without repercussion and find your voice
Your mentee is struggling with many issues; you worry you lack the skills to help them	Sometime it is enough to listen, to act as a sounding board. You are not always there to provide an answer, but to help the mentee arrive at one. If you feel the issue is beyond your scope then signpost to another professional, for example, a counsellor	Your mentor is an expert in your field and has clever and helpful ideas which you have used. You have been congratulated for them	You should learn from your mentor but remember that they should be acknowledged for their work. The main purpose of mentoring is to help you develop your own concepts and have the confidence to promote them

Symptoms and causes

There are a number of symptoms that can point to the presence of toxicity. In a US study of 277 senior to top level managers participating in an executive development programme (Eby, McManus, Simon and Russell, 2000), eighty-four had experienced at least one unfavourable mentoring experience, including mismatching, distancing, manipulative behaviours and lack of expertise. Causal factors identified included the mentor's motives for engagement, ineffective matching and monitoring, poor mentoring scheme design and inadequate safeguards. Other causes for toxicity can range from mentor burnout to mentor negative affect (Eby, Durley, Evans and Ragins, 2008) where the mentor has a tendency to present a negative world viewpoint. Subtler causes include counter-transference, where the mentor can be unwittingly influenced by the mentee's own feelings expressed through non-verbal behaviours (Lee, 2010).

Eby (2007: 323) categorised three different severity levels: low, moderate and high, associated with mentoring problems with recurring themes such as mismatches, mentor neglect, skills shortages, manipulation, expectations and boundary violations. Yet perceptions of experiences can be subjective, for example, the unmet expectations identified as low severity in Eby's study were recorded as causing high toxic impact in another study (Washington 2016).

Simon and Eby's (2003) study of negative experiences is one of few to perceive a difference between mentoring models in terms of toxicity experienced. They linked career-related mentoring with toxicity where, for example, the mentor lacked the technical skills to help the mentee, and associated toxicity in psycho-social mentoring with poor interpersonal skills. Hamlin and Sage (2011) established that many of the criteria in their model of positive mentoring effectiveness were consistent with Megginson et al.'s (2006) developmental mentoring model. They noted that successful relationships were reliant not only on the competence of the mentor but the behaviour of the mentee, and recommended awareness sessions for the dyad to understand expectations and roles.

What these studies clearly demonstrate is the presence of common themes and patterns of behaviour that correlate with problems encountered in the mentoring relationship. This knowledge delivers powerful insight into what is going wrong and where to concentrate efforts to safeguard the process, substantiating the importance of assessment and research.

The problems identified in the course of research can be ascribed to either systemic or interpersonal issues or sometimes both. Those of a systemic nature relate to how mentoring is designed and organised or the model adopted. Lack of mentor technical knowledge (rather than actual mentoring skills), for instance, is more pertinent to the traditional model than to developmental mentoring. These can be addressed by reviewing the mechanics of the scheme itself.

Toxic features of an interpersonal nature present more complex obstacles as they are often subject to the vagaries of individual disposition. Differences in culture, values and personality together with conflicting roles or status and the chemistry between the participants need to be respected and managed. These interpersonal issues should be tackled through matching, contracting and training (see chapter 5).

There is a relationship between lack of motivation and emotional intelligence. Ragins (2009: 243–7) linked motivation to positive self-representation which she argued created positive relationships. There are components of self-structures – beliefs about oneself – that particularly influence mentoring. Positive self-structures have a role in the prevention of toxicity. The first component: relational identity, describes the regard individuals attach to themselves in the mentoring relationship. Whether the identity is deemed positive or negative will have an ongoing effect on behaviours. The second component relates to mentoring schemas: maps based on past experiences, which may influence current decisions or actions. The final component consists of possible selves – either positive or negative, reflecting the desired self or the feared self, which, again, can influence behaviour. Ragins associates this self-representation with strategic emotional management using frameworks, such as mindfulness and emotional intelligence, and skills, such as emotion regulation and self-narration: the formation of identity through story. Studies also suggest a connection exists between positive emotions and resilience.

The incidence and impact of toxicity is also influenced by the level of emotional intelligence in the dyad or the resilience of the mentee (Tugade and Fredrickson, 2004). Emotionally intelligent mentoring guards against toxicity and can be an effective treatment for toxic relationships. It is even possible to transform negative experiences into development opportunities, or re-shape a toxic relationship into a successful one, rather than simply abandoning it. Tugade and Fredrickson explain how the use of positive emotions manufacture a positive outcome from a negative situation. The extent to which emotional intelligence influences the effectiveness of mentoring is significant.

Summary

While toxic events may never be completely eliminated, they can be minimised. Raising awareness of helpful behaviours through orientation sessions, ongoing training and development offers an effective safeguard. The application of interventions such as emotional intelligence development can prevent a weak relationship from deteriorating into a destructive one. Regularly reviewing the mentoring contract also provides a health check of the relationship to prevent vexations escalating into an irreconcilable collapse.

CHAPTER TIPS

- Be toxic-aware, discuss the possibility of toxicity in the initial contract and how you will react as a team to deal with it.
- Reflect upon your own conduct and be mindful of unhelpful behaviours.
- Develop the dyad's emotional intelligence and resilience by practicing open, constructive feedback.
- Maintain a positive attitude.
- Play the critical friend so you are not afraid of difficult conversations. They are an opportunity to clear the air, refreshing and strengthening the relationship.
- Avoid the blame game.

Understanding why and how toxicity interferes with the mentoring process is complex, and it is a subject worthy of further investigation. Its existence should not be allowed to detract from the positive aspects of mentoring but awareness of the threat is often sufficient to head it off before it takes hold of the relationship. As with any poison it is a question of finding an appropriate antidote.

CHAPTER 5
Mentoring Schemes

This chapter features the primary requirements for setting up a structured mentoring scheme. The qualities of a mentor are considered, along with the impact of expectations and motivation. The content is predominantly aimed at larger mentoring schemes that possess sufficient resources to fully implement the concepts put forward and which, because of their size, require more robust and structured administrative organisation. The principles, however, are just as pertinent to smaller schemes but may require a little creative thinking to minimise the burden where resources are limited.

An evaluation of the areas most relevant to needs may identify unnecessary features or the possibility of combining functions.

Each section of this chapter covers a specific element of the considerations needed to create the ideal scheme. Some can be addressed by asking a few simple questions.

Objective

First, ask yourself these questions:

- Why do you want/need this scheme?
- What are the desired outcomes?
- Who is it aimed at?

A reasonable starting point for any scheme is to establish its aims, objectives, values and ethos. This will help in the choice of the most suitable model to install. If the need is to support a business where the owner is planning retirement, the scheme focus may be on career development to generate sustainability and resilience through effective succession planning. Stepping back to scrutinise the roles within the business, who occupies them and what action would be needed should the individual leave, would identify others who could fill it and where any risks are exposed. These can then be addressed through mentoring activities such as job shadowing to ensure that succession planning is robust and trouble-free.

It may be that a graduate scheme is required to initiate new intakes to the organisational culture and to internally grow the next generation of leaders. There may be a need to address a specific issue, high rates of absence, for example, and aim, through mentoring, to instil feelings of value, appreciation and development in the workforce. The various sub-modalities of mentoring should also be considered; perhaps the equality of peer mentoring would work best, or a business mentoring method – more aggressive in nature – is needed, or executive mentoring with its customised approach.

Above all, it is vital to be aware of the cultural dynamics of the group participating in the scheme, and to be sensitive to these influences to avoid erecting barriers to success (Kent et al., 2013). An example of this would be to consider culture and values when matching a dyad; a female mentor may be able to relate more helpfully to a female mentee in terms of common challenges faced, for instance.

Operation

While establishing the objectives clarifies the framework needed for its operation, putting together a mentoring scheme then requires other questions to be posed. How will it work? What resources are needed? Who will run it? The word 'how' might seem uncomplicated but finding the answer is far more demanding.

Practicalities are invariably the driving consideration in the design of schemes. Where its administration is managed centrally, perhaps by a department such as Human Resources and included within an existing role, the appointment of a coordinator may be unnecessary and therefore a mentee self-select system is more pragmatic. This can work well, where a part-time coordinator can advise or intervene as appropriate. Delivered training could also be dispensed with so long as comprehensive written guidance is made available to the dyad. However, where resources have been allocated, a dedicated coordinator and adequate training provision made, outcomes are measurably improved. This is more often the case in a decentralised system where operational management of the scheme is devolved within the organisation while strategic policy is retained centrally.

Innovations in information technology offer alternative dimensions, such as virtual mentoring, allowing remote worldwide interaction with expert mentors (Colky and Young,

2006). It enables convenient communicating across geographical distance eliminating any mobility restrictions, facilitating ready accessibility to the mentor and avoiding time constraints or the need for meetings. Whatever the medium, empathic communication skills still need to be maintained to prevent misunderstanding of message tone and meaning. While online programmes can be very effective. Honey (2007) warns that e-learning is rarely successful unless backed by full commitment from the participants. Technology can greatly enhance virtual mentoring processes: examples include instant messaging, email, video-conferencing and discussion groups – all systems that are accessible within a large organisation. Adopting such a strategy can help overcome lack of time issues which are a commonly acknowledged constraint. E-mentoring is also meeting proof, time zone friendly and unrestricted by venue.

Harnessing these technologies also offers a wider service to mentoring schemes by supporting essential components such as matching dyads, defining relationship boundaries and establishing expectations. Scheme guidelines and mentoring advice can be easily accessed online. A database of mentors, specifying contact details, expectations, outcomes, geographical area, experience and the type of support offered, and whether conducted remotely or in person, is usually sufficient information for the would-be mentee to identify a potentially successful dyad. It should be kept in mind, however, that these data are useful only if kept up to date, and it is essential that care is taken over issues of confidentiality and privacy.

While remote training can be successful, it does deprive the association of the advantages of networking with other scheme members to promote belonging and generate enthusiasm for the mentoring activity. Combining networking events with training and development can either be elaborate with invited expert speakers, or kept relatively simple and cost effective through regular action learning sets where members can meet and share experiences, learning from each other in the process.

Selling the idea

Winning support for a mentoring scheme proposal is likely to be influenced by responses to a further set of questions:

- What will it cost?
- Who will fund it?
- Who makes the decisions?
- How should the business case be pitched?

The financial implications will be inevitably dependent upon the scale and scope of the proposed scheme. It would, however, need to address the routine essentials for any new start-up initiative: calculating costings for staff, accommodation, equipment, training, marketing and materials. The case itself needs to be delivered from two perspectives: the organisation and the members, and justifying the expenditure of time and funds can be challenging. However, the scheme costs can be adjusted according to the budget available. A good approach is to start with a comprehensive ideal, then, by judicious pruning and cherry-picking of essentials, settle on an appropriate blueprint. The flexibility of mentoring allows an impressive array of options. It is also wise to offer one or two alternatives to the preferred option, setting out the cost benefits of each. A single option proposal risks the loss of the whole concept should it be considered too ambitious. Stakeholders often defer to return on investment when taking such decisions.

Reinforcing justification through reference to published research immediately adds validity and weight to an argument and there is plenty of choice on studies demonstrating the business advantages of mentoring. For example, a study of formal mentoring for female leaders (Høigaard and Mathisen, 2009) revealed that participants experienced increased job satisfaction, career planning and perceived leadership behaviour. Kennett and Lomas's study (2015) found that mentoring improves employee engagement by providing meaning at work, benefiting not only mentors and mentees but also the organisation.

Scheme coordination

The role of coordinator often goes unnoticed yet can be vital to a scheme's success. A good coordinator needs to be a good organiser, an effective communicator, a mediator and possess good analytical skills. Experience can be wide-ranging but not necessarily directly connected to mentoring. A professional involved in staff development, administration or management, for example, can bring a range of skills appropriate to the role. An interest or belief in the benefits of mentoring is important to establish a strong ethos throughout the scheme and set the tone for its members.

While such a role may only be sustainable in schemes involving large numbers of mentors and mentees, bypassing it could, in the long term, however, prove costly and initiatives may fail in the absence of a driving force behind them. In its comprehensive form, the responsibilities of a fully functional scheme coordinator are manifold. They include:

- a full understanding of the system adopted and the policies underpinning it
- identifying potential mentors and promoting the scheme to mentees
- matching of mentees with mentors
- organising training and information materials
- coordination of the scheme and maintaining records
- controlling the budget

- acting as a link between its members and stakeholders
- arbitrating on ethical issues and generally mediating for the dyad.

Once again, the nature of the role will vary somewhat in accordance with the scope of the programme adopted.

Finding your mentors

As mentioned earlier, some organisations appoint mentors as part of their job role then assign mentees to them, in which case the coordinator merely acts to facilitate this. Under the voluntary arrangement greater effort and ingenuity is needed in the search for suitable mentors. This demands that the idea is sold to the workforce as well as to management.

Daloz (1999) notes how mentors emerge out of the need of the moment. However, rather than rely on such a responsive 'fire-fighting' approach, it would be more powerful to deliberately and systematically engage staff in the process pre-emptively. Taking proactive action is key to its success.

The first steps in the quest to find mentors involve looking internally by 'trawling' the organisation and using publicity by promoting the scheme through events, newsletters and staff magazines. As the word spreads engagement follows.

If potential numbers do not warrant proceeding or costs are too high, consider negotiating a joint venture with other existing or proposed schemes that might fit the bill. Most functioning schemes use a website so can be readily identified through an internet search. This expands the pool of mentors and shares any financial burden. Concessions to some of your proposed working arrangements can be made without compromising overall aims and objectives. There are many examples of successful collaboration in the public sector but it can also work in the commercial world provided there are no conflicts of interest.

Exploiting existing organisational dynamics to build impetus for forming a working body of mentors can produce impressive results. This is demonstrated to good effect by the Metropolitan Police Resources Personnel Development Unit (2004: 44) which delivered mentoring courses to staff so that they could go on to form a 'Network of Mentors'. Participants were taught the requisites for being an effective mentor and the scheme was then advertised so that staff could match with a mentor. This proved successful and was adopted by other units creating a cascade effect through the organisation. This is a good example of cascade mentoring utilising change agents within an organisation. A change agent is a team member who carries influence with the group. Everard and Morris (2004) recommend promoting such schemes to the change agents beforehand, giving impetus to changes before any resistance is accumulated. The risk of failure to comprehend the meaning of mentoring or the benefits it could accord could be averted through the use of change agents.

Matching

Prescribed matching has been criticised for imposing a relationship that should occur naturally, i.e. the dyad drawn to each other independent of the organisation or scheme requirements (Allen, Finkelstein and Poteet 2012). Some schemes do allow the mentee to self-select on the strength of mentor biographies, highlighting professional, sector or mentor experience that appeals to the mentee. Others allow partial selection which may present parameters such as seniority level but without appointing specific mentors. The selection of a mentor identified as a role model can work well if it is the mentee's choice (Cox, 2005). Research has found that specific matching of, for example, ethnicity, can be valuable (Campbell and Campbell, 2007), but in its general use any clear-cut benefits of choosing your own mentor remains unproven.

Some schemes attach particular emphasis on the matching process. The Women in Universities Mentoring Scheme (WUMS), for example, matches dyads anonymously by applying standard criteria before the final adjudication by a Match Review Panel (WUMS, 2010). Some studies have concluded that such considered matching is more effective at securing successful outcomes. Parker (2010) examined the effect of matching on teacher retention in a quantitative study, finding that those who had been purposefully matched were more likely to remain with the organisation. However, Cox's (2005) qualitative research of a community mentoring project suggests that matching is more complex. It reveals that the underlying needs of the mentee do not fully emerge until after the relationship has formed and can change over time, invalidating the initial matching and potentially channelling the mentee in an inappropriate direction.

In their paper on setting up a mentoring scheme, Coll and Raghavan (2011) promote matching against preset selection criteria, ensuring that mentors are both voluntary and meet the criterion. Mentees must similarly satisfy qualifying requirements determined by organisational policy objectives. In contrast, in their case study of a peer mentoring programme, Fleck and Mullins (2012) concluded that initial dyad compatibility was not a proven necessity.

The debate remains unresolved on the best way to match and its relevance to successful outcomes for the dyad is, in the main, inconclusive. Some innovative approaches have been tried such as speed mentoring – similar to the speed dating concept – where mentee and mentor spend a brief time together to gauge compatibility.

Resolving how best to proceed needs therefore to be based on individual judgement or organisational necessity and practicability. Table 6 offers a simplistic overview of the matching process but as with many aspects of mentoring the approach can be blended or adapted to inject the values and intent desired.

Table 6: ELEMENTS OF A MENTORING MATCHING PROCESS

Action	Specification
Mentee selects from standard criteria and provides a brief statement explaining why they want a mentor	Communicating aspirations, motivation, experience and expectations
Mentor submits biography	Including experience, expertise, motivation, expectations and prior mentoring training
Scheme coordinator identifies potential match and provides contact details	Mentee contacts Mentor to initiate first meeting
Scheme coordinator provides ongoing support	Dyad is responsible for the ongoing success of the relationship through the creation and revisiting of a mentoring contract

Training

Effective training for both mentor and mentee is pivotal to mentoring success. Many schemes offer initial training, and some continue to provide networking events with relevant speakers, masterclasses and opportunities to enhance mentoring skills. The North West Leadership Academy, for example, applies this to good effect. The more active the scheme is in engagement the more successful it is likely to be. Training is often voluntary or mentors may be exempt through mentoring expertise gained previously. Yet training should not be restricted to ensuring that mentors possess the appropriate skills. It should also be an opportunity to introduce the dyad to the scheme: its aims and objectives, its ethos, its culture, and imbue in them a sense of belonging, to promote active and positive participation. Compulsory training and engagement in ongoing events broadcasts a clear message of responsibility and fellowship.

Appropriate training is an increasingly relevant influence on the mentoring industry as it becomes more predominant as the treatment of choice for a broader range of societal issues. Some perceive that the only quality needed to be a mentor is experience but there is a general recognition that some kind of education and expertise is necessary in the pursuit of mentoring excellence. At the very least, it can provide orientation for the scheme (Megginson et al., 2006). Elements of mentoring appear in a range of broader teaching and management courses but initiation into a scheme still warrants some form of induction to instil a lasting, positive influence.

A directory of validated courses offers a useful guide to ensure that advice given is of an adequate standard. Educational mentoring programmes are on the increase in the academic field with such courses as the foundation degree in Coaching and Mentoring or the BA (Hons) in Teaching, Learning and Mentoring along with shorter, focused training courses and modules. A plethora of learning materials is also available that can be adapted for individual programmes (Learning Wales, 2015). Wallace and Gravells (2007) supported the case for training to ensure comprehension of responsibilities and to address issues such as ethical considerations. The provision of an institution-specific training course would ensure that each mentor had the same starting point with a clear understanding of their role in relation to the organisation.

While several of the causes of toxicity, outlined in chapter 4, could be related to failures in understanding, full appreciation of the impact of training on outcomes is limited and further research into this area would be useful. A more detailed qualitative assessment of mentors through interviews would establish if there was a relationship between lack of qualification in the mentor and the positive or negative experience of the mentee.

Ongoing development should also be actively encouraged as Boyatzis (2007: 454) warns that the 'honeymoon effect' of a training programme might show behavioural improvement initially, but without nurture it could quickly dissipate. Masterclasses exploring new or more advanced techniques and seminars with specialist speakers and networking events will strengthen any scheme and encourage participation and growth. Even by promoting it as a proud organisational benefit could attract new talent to the workforce.

Contractual prerequisites

One of the most important steps in ensuring a successful mentoring relationship is to enter into a contract which represents the skeletal structure for the relationship before it is 'fleshed out' as the dyad flourishes. The bones of this skeleton are detailed in the following sections but it is first helpful to review some of the more basic obligations. The mentoring connection is one centred on trust within the dyad which to be secured, needs the two parties to commit to and comply with the prerequisites of each role.

The Mentor

The two broad mentor functions of either sponsorship (based on the mentor's senior position in the organisation), or psychosocial (focusing on interpersonal development) were identified by Kram in 1985 and later corroborated by Higgins, Chandler and Kram in 2007. This work was subsequently refined (Scandura and Viator, 1994; Ensher and Murphy, 1997) with a further classification, role modelling, added to that of sponsorship and psychosocial. In order to deliver the variety of benefits on offer, mentors must first have clear understanding of the styles of support available.

It is the mentor's responsibility to ensure that the mentee has a realistic and appropriate expectation of what they can achieve through the process. Misaligned expectations can lead to toxicity and therefore continuous checks are needed to ensure that the dyad remains simpatico and in accord.

Adopting a reflective practitioner attitude within the mentoring process is an effective mentoring quality. Reflection is learning by experience and the reflective process can be described in three stages: remembering the experience, awareness of associated feelings and re-evaluating the experience (Boud, Keough, and Walker, 1985). This combination reinforces understanding and contributes towards learning and, ultimately, growth. Identifying development needs using this process may, for example, lead to training thus developing the individual who should in turn deliver a more valuable contribution to the organisation. Encouraging such professional reflection is an important, facilitative role of a mentor and should form the foundation of the relationship.

Important skills and qualities in a mentor, outlined in chapter 2, include the ability to listen, to interpret non-verbal signals and ask well-timed questions that provoke thought and reflection. A mentor should also be aware of the responsibility and privilege conferred upon them. They may well represent a significant influence in the mentee's world which should neither be viewed lightly nor leave the mentor awestruck at the potential power. The role should be approached with a calm determination to help and support the mentee to the best of their ability.

The motivation to mentor can encompass a range of reasons. Many mentors are drawn to the activity for altruistic intentions, a desire to give something back, to make a difference. Equally, many mentors are attracted by the opportunities for development that participation may offer, or even to strengthen promotional prospects through raising their profile within the organisation. Less benevolent or more self-serving motivation does not necessarily make a poor mentor. The mentee may be seen as a reflection of the mentor and therefore a successful mentee will complement both and be regarded with satisfaction by all concerned.

The Mentee

The role of the mentee should not be a passive one. Without proactive engagement a mentor will struggle to successfully support their mentee. The mentee must 'sign up' to the mentoring process and without their cooperation and enthusiasm for learning the relationship is likely to fail.

The mentee may enter the relationship with high hopes and expectations, and these can be unrealistic. They may view the mentor as the guru with all the answers to solve all their problems. This can put undue pressure on the mentor and in setting a more workable tone it is a wise mentor who reveals their fallible human side. The process should be promoted as a team effort; the idea of two brains being better than one render the assumption of infallibility less potent leading to a more relaxed and realistic environment.

The most valuable attribute for an effective mentee is commitment. Appreciating the time and effort invested by a mentor by embracing the responsibilities of a mentee is the highest compliment. A mentee should be dedicated to their own progression and take a proactive approach to ideas and strategies considered in the mentoring process. They should respect arrangements made for meetings, avoid tardiness and adopt an open mind and heart.

Motivation represents a key trait for the mentee. Why do they want mentoring? Do they, in fact, want it, or have they been obliged – perhaps by a manager – to engage in it. Enforced mentoring can be challenging for the mentor but the obstacles need not be insurmountable. It is a rare individual who needs no mentoring, guidance or advice in terms of development; it is simply a matter of uncovering how they can be helped. If it is acknowledged that a mentee has been obliged to participate, it can then be argued that they may as well engage with the process to establish whether there are any benefits for them. The mentor should then make use of open questions to encourage the mentee to tell their story. It is unlikely that no opportunities for either development, reflection or problem solving would surface given sufficient time. Simply giving the mentee an opportunity to talk, unencumbered, in a safe environment often results in the most powerful exchanges.

The mentoring contract

The mentoring process is governed by an agreement between the mentor and mentee. Known as contracting, it provides a narrative of intent and behaviour that gives the mentoring strategy appropriate direction. This is not a contract in the legal sense, and although it sounds quite formal it does not need to be as it is essentially a vehicle for understanding how the sessions will work and an opportunity to ascertain each other's expectations and hopes for the association. It can be written or verbal but if written it must be stored securely to protect the confidentiality of both parties. It should be revisited periodically to ensure the relationship continues to suit the dyad and still provide a positive and rewarding experience for both. The contract should be as comprehensive as possible and agreed at the outset:

1. *The Practicalities*
   a. Where will you meet?
   Where mentoring occurs in the workplace, is this the best environment for a mentoring conversation? Is there a likelihood of interruption? Will the mentee feel relaxed and able to confide? It may well be suitable but the question is worth asking and an alternative location, perhaps away from work such as a coffee bar may garner a more relaxed and open exchange.

b. How often will you meet?

This, as with all contract criteria, is up to the dyad. On average, a monthly meeting to plan forward or review would suffice, but it is entirely at the discretion of the dyad and should be centred on mentee need.

c. How long should it take?

A mentoring conversation is focused and therefore tiring, so approximately an hour would be manageable, certainly no more than two. Less than an hour may indicate a lack of engagement or question the need for the meetings. It is also important that both mentor and mentee allow time in their diaries before the meeting to prepare and focus and after the meeting to reflect upon what was said. The mentee should reflect on what was explored and any action to be undertaken and the mentor may use the time to consider how they mentored: whether they listened effectively, or if the questions they asked were timely and helpful to the mentee.

d. How will you contact each other?

Some may be comfortable with sharing personal mobile phone contacts or prefer business email exchange. A mentor may equally be happy for the mentee to contact them late in the evening. However, it should be kept in mind that this is workplace mentoring. Mentoring should be used to plan ahead and prepare for an event or activity and then to review and reflect upon it afterwards; there should be no mentoring emergencies!

2. *Expectations*

One of the main causes of toxicity in mentoring is mismatched expectations. The mentee may expect a developmental mentor to be more directive and take the lead in discussions, or the mentor may presume that the mentee will arrange and coordinate meetings. Clearly establishing each other's perceptions and hopes prevents later difficulties. Assumptions should be avoided and every aspect tackled in a detailed and open contract without rules. There is no prescribed way to conduct a mentoring experience, only the right way for both, and how that looks can only be determined through the construction of a robust contract. What does mentoring mean to you? What do you expect? What is acceptable to you? What do you want from it? Exploring these fundamental questions can be challenging but sets the tone for a professional exchange which meets each other's needs and hopes.

3. *Conduct*

   a. Structure

Adherence to a structure for the mentoring session avoids it slipping into a mere chat. It is the mentor's responsibility to guide the process and ensure it remains on track, and there are various approaches that can be utilised to provide that structure. For example, a popular coaching system is GROW which sets four stages to the exchange: identifying a Goal, the mentee describes the current Reality or situation, the dyad explore various Options allowing the mentee to commit to action, and finally demonstrates the Will to pursue it. Structural composition is flexible and varied but following any kind of framework is helpful.

A standard form of structure works like this:
   i.   at the beginning of every meeting establish the goal for the session
   ii.   allow the mentee time and space to fully explain the story behind the goal
   iii. discuss a range of options
   iv.   allow the mentee to identify which one to try. This increases ownership and the likelihood of the mentee's commitment to it
   v.   plan the execution of the option
   vi.   review the session and arrange the next one.

This structure may be applied over more than one session depending on mentee need.

b. Confidentiality

Confidentiality is vital to the success of the relationship. Both mentor and mentee need to know that the mentoring space and their exchanges are secure. The mentee will be more open in such an environment; delivering deeper, adventurous exploration and more creative solutions becomes less likely if the mentee is concerned that the information will leave the room. It presents a challenge for the mentor to distance themselves from, for example, their knowledge of individuals mentioned or organisational politics. Conversely, it is equally important that the mentor has faith in the mentee not to talk about them.

Issues of confidentiality should be addressed at an early stage of the mentoring contract and feature as a gentle reminder at every other session. It represents an ongoing bilateral commitment and should be viewed in earnest. As it is the foundation upon which the entire structure is built, when threatened it can signal a most unsatisfactory end. There are, of course, exceptions to most rules and the caveat here would be if a mentee was considered to be in danger of harming themselves or others, break the law, or in any way threaten the mentor's ethical code; likewise if there were similar concerns about the mentor. This should be explained during initial discussions and best done with a light touch to avoid any discomfort or unfounded anxieties.

Any concern should be highlighted and discussed, appropriate help and support offered or signposted and the troubled individual persuaded to act, on the understanding that their partner may be forced to do so otherwise. This dramatic occurrence is rare and would represent a significant adjustment or even end the relationship. However, if a mentee was in danger of harming themselves, obtaining appropriate professional help would override all else before mentoring could be resumed.

c. Finishing

Planning a satisfactory ending to the relationship is as important as planning its beginning. Relationships left to drift and founder often leave behind unresolved issues and feelings of discontent. It is vital to recognise when the relationship is approaching a natural conclusion, then reflect together, reviewing its successes and challenges and celebrating the association. When drawing up your contract discuss how you will recognise this important stage and plan for it.

4. *Boundaries*

Boundaries constitute the limits of acceptable conversation or behaviour to both mentor and mentee. It represents where the line is drawn and if it is crossed. Establishing the parameters of the relationship naturally include ethical discussions such as professional and moral codes.

Both mentor and mentee, for example, could be vulnerable to exploitation. It is the responsibility of the organisation to ensure that the dyad is appropriately protected and fully aware of its ethical responsibilities. Bolton (2001) observed the risks in a dyad within a shared place of work posing a potential threat of exposing confidential information about colleagues or clients, for example, knowledge of poor practice or inappropriate behaviour.

Moral codes may be applied to unacceptable behaviours, both legal and personal, involving inappropriate or overfamiliar behaviour by either party's standards. It is useful to raise such issues at the contracting stage. Establishing a safe word, phrase or sign to indicate that either is unhappy or uncomfortable can diffuse situations quickly. It doesn't need to be covert, simply agree that if either mentions or does anything causing concern to say, 'Let's change the subject' or 'This isn't working for me'. Merely pointing out the behaviour, for example, 'I would prefer you not to sit so close', or 'I am not happy with you referring to this' would be sufficient. Should a boundary breach be identified, agreeing that the imposer should desist either with or without an explanation can also be constructive. Any ongoing discussion or exploration of the behaviour or the reason it caused distress should be regarded as a development opportunity. The ideal dyad should feel sufficiently confident to raise and discuss such potentially awkward issues; mentoring is after all an opportunity for not only the mentee to grow but also for the mentor.

5. *Reviewing the Contract*
   Relationships change over time as the mentee's needs develop and evolve. To ensure continuing positive benefits, it is helpful to review the mentoring contract either following a breakthrough or a goal achieved or intermittently every few months. Setting aside regular review meetings gauges the temperature of the connection, to verify that rapport is still strong, that boundaries remain relevant and the association endures as positive and helpful. Minor adjustments as you progress can help avoid difficulties or misunderstandings and reinvigorate the link to prevent mentoring fatigue.

Assessment

The evaluation and monitoring of formal mentoring programmes assures continued quality and improved practice. Informal mentoring is popular but impractical to monitor, and in the absence of assessment it is impossible to objectively measure benefits. Formative evaluation, conducted during the relationship, is a vital element of the mentoring process to review progress and understanding and to encourage reflection. Summative evaluation, following completion of the relationship, supplies useful information on the success of a programme and where improvement is required. It also provides an indicator for the feasibility of the dyad or whether the mentor requires further training.

Any evaluative process needs to be carefully conducted and sensitive to privacy issues. Mentoring is, by nature, a confidential practice and protection of the dyad must remain paramount. Maintaining anonymity in monitoring is therefore advisable. Both parties need to be aware of any codes and procedures laid down by the organisation and how these relate to national codes and to the law itself, such as data protection should any records be produced.

The measurement of mentoring success, however, is stubbornly problematic and a uniform model for evaluation remains elusive. In one study (Gaskell, 2007) only a third of organisations were able to successfully measure the impact of coaching, despite the availability of adequate resources and substantial investment in the programmes. Demonstrating ROI (return on investment) for enterprises employing soft skills can be equally challenging, particularly when endeavouring to separate the mentoring aspect from other factors influencing personal development. Establishing ROE (return on expectation) is, however, a more manageable proposition and can prove valuable. Some efforts to identify the impact of professional development interventions have generated some innovative approaches such as the 'isolation factor' identified in research by McGovern, Lindemann, Vergara, Murphy, Barker and Warrenfeltz (2001). This study separates out the effects of coaching but its conclusions were derived purely from the perspective of the participants and, arguably, lacks robust objectivity. Regardless of how success is measured, the popularity of mentoring continues to grow and its benefits widely appreciated.

Some form of monitoring and assessment is advisable to ensure a scheme is productive and efficacious. The challenge is how to accomplish this while protecting the confidentiality of a process based on trust so that anything shared is respected and safeguarded. Mentoring can improve recruitment, retention and development of staff, but potential risks such as problems arising from mismatched relationships, undefined boundaries subject to subsequent challenge, rivalry within the dyads and motivational risks exist. All these threats can be ameliorated by the appropriate training of participants and the formulation of clear guidelines both for the process itself and what is expected of each party. The absence of discrete monitoring makes it harder to guard against abuses, such as breach of confidentiality, or ensuring participants are maximising potential benefits. Such evaluation could include a confidential and anonymous feedback process. Even a record of attendance could indicate a prognostic opinion of arising issues, whereby erratic participation by the mentee may suggest a breakdown in the dyad which could then be addressed. There is a compelling case for affording comprehensible guidelines and support at all stages within a formal framework.

Reluctance to assess such programmes stems from a widely held principle that the very essence of mentoring demands a confidential relationship. Incorporating assessment into an established confidential framework, such as staff appraisal systems, could provide the solution. This knowledge would deliver vital data that could be compared to, for example, absence records or staff turnover to establish patterns or links to determine the influence of mentoring on the organisation.

Success

How will you demonstrate success?

Transforming evaluation and monitoring data into publishable research that could be presented at conferences and seminars is a respected route to market your scheme, bringing validity and esteem which reflects upon its hosting organisation. Building such a reputation has additional benefits for a business such as attracting talent to work there. Celebrating success through networking events and award ceremonies provides the opportunity to recognise effort, commitment and aptitude as well as radiate a positive perception of the organisation.

Summary

The genesis of human actions begins with an idea and the question 'why?' Once that has been established the idea can be 'fleshed out' with other pertinent questions: How? Who? When? What? Resolving these questions establishes the theoretical framework for realising the idea, providing a clarification that simplifies the formulation of the practical components. While this resilient blueprint yields a sound foundation for creating a mentoring scheme, it is only through progressive evolution and refinement that it will remain 'fit for purpose'.

CHAPTER TIPS

If tasked with setting up a mentoring scheme for your organisation you may feel quite overwhelmed at the prospect. Often this demand will accompany an existing role and you will be expected to simply find the time. View this as an opportunity that could grow and become a key element of your role and provide you with the chance to introduce and develop a showboat initiative for your organisation.

Enlisting support for your scheme will seal enthusiasm and secure additional resources. Prepare a professional presentation and 'sell' it at the highest level. Make it business-focused with research statistics at hand, and drive home all the benefits culminating in financial advantages. For example, mentoring increases staff satisfaction, influencing productivity, elevating sales and increasing profit. If you can recruit an executive level advocate who will promote and sponsor your scheme at the top, this could lead to organisational commitment, increasing the likelihood of the longevity, growth and success of the scheme.

CHAPTER 6
Distal Mentoring

The distal mentoring concept is rooted in the principles of developmental mentoring but with evolutionary adaptations intended to reduce the incidence of toxicity. The distal aspect expresses a mentoring relationship transformation over a period of time through co-participatory approaches at a distance. This distance is not restricted to geographical detachment but more from the standpoint of occupational separation, allowing the mentor to be drawn from outside the mentee's profession or organisation. The mentor/mentee matching can then be made on the basis of personal compatibility to generate a team association with an equal division of power.

The onus on the mentor is to listen rather than serve up instant advice and to encourage the mentee to explore and create solutions. By not knowing the mentee's organisation or the characters in the mentee's world, there is no temptation to engage the mentee's manager or colleagues, no need to participate or be influenced by the organisation's politics, no opportunity for self-gain or promotion.

As explained in earlier chapters, successful mentoring demands the procurement of sufficient expertise based on the possession of emotional intelligence and self-regard and be congruent with mentees. This is integral to the distal approach and, by removing the need for specialist knowledge, provides the opportunity for evolving mentoring as a field into a cross organisational, cross professional resource, thereby creating unrestricted access to the available pool of mentoring dyads. This unique element of distal mentoring sustains confidentiality and elevates the assurance of trust within the relationship.

There is a case for more directive mentoring in organisations where specific procedures need to be followed or passed on, whereas the developmental style of the distal model is more gainful in sectors that require creativity. It serves as an inspiration for fresh ideas, encouraging innovation and fashions a more rounded individual capable of lateral thinking.

The distal approach also lends itself well to the utilisation of technological advances through e-communication and social media with boundaries only limited by internet connection. General use of such facilities is now widespread and for many is the preferred means of maintaining contact because of its speed, convenience and low cost. It presents the opportunity to expand horizons through national or international collaboration.

Taking the e-mentoring route must come with a degree of caution. It is best avoided if the interaction is restricted to e-mail or similar keyboard communication as the absence of non-verbal pointers such as facial expression or body language and voice intonation loses many of the mentor insights and is open to misinterpretation. However, this may be partially diminished using audio-visual communication devices. Despite the limitations the system still has much to offer provided both mentor and mentee are competent and confident of adopting this approach.

The distal model

The distal model has its origins in the Megginson et al. (2006) developmental mentoring model (see chapter 3) which was utilised in a major regional public services scheme involving the participation of sixty four separate bodies with a mentoring membership of 2132. Its members were encouraged to form mentoring dyads beyond their own organisation to support confidentiality and protect against ethical concerns. The collaboration also provided a cost-effective funding solution through the sharing of administrative costs and the training of mentors and mentees.

A case study of the scheme (Washington, 2013) examined experiences of toxicity amongst both mentors and mentees. As a result of its findings, each phase of the scheme's model was analysed to specifically target the incidence of toxicity attributed to systemic failures and to address the interpersonal triggers outlined in chapter 4. The review also considered the significance of its constituent elements by reflecting on current usage, thinking and understanding of the mentoring process. While most aspects of Megginson's five-phase model remain the same, the re-emphasis of individual components deemed to have a distinguishable impact, particularly in the face of toxic influence, has warranted some remodelling and amplification by the inclusion of an additional stage:

- phase one: contracting and building the relationship
- phase two: understanding
- phase three: analysis and challenge
- phase four: options and action planning
- phase five: review and implementation
- phase six: detachment and celebration

Built on Kram's (1983) original four-stage sponsorship model and Megginson et al.'s (2006) five-phase developmental model the design aims to protect against the issues uncovered by the case study (Washington, 2013). To strengthen protection from toxicity the distal model extends the developmental model to six phases to deal with the risk of unresolved endings and allowing elements of the other phases to be re-informed. The first phase still retains the essential features of contracting, utilising rapport-building skills. Empathic listening guides phase two, focusing purely on understanding the mentee's worldview. This differs from the previous models which require goals to be set at this point. Phase three, as with the other models, analyses the situation using compassionate challenge techniques where appropriate. While phase four in the developmental model covers the winding up process, the distal model discusses a range of options culminating in an action plan for the mentee to implement. The fifth and final phase for the developmental model relating to 'winding up and moving on' is where the distal model reviews the implementation. The additional sixth phase is dedicated solely to achieving a satisfactory conclusion, redefining the relationship ensuring that both parties may move on with no unresolved issues. It would address any toxicity, negativity or misunderstanding that may have occurred during the association. Its success, however, is dependent on the dyad concluding the phase in accordance with the initial contract which can only be achieved by attaching some endorsement to the process, if only through completion of a form to confirm that all phases had been undertaken. This reporting back ensures that the dyad does not merely fade away.

The distal model is therefore more detailed, providing distinct phases to each element, possibly slowing down the process. However, mentoring should not be a quick fix and such a reflective model needs time and space to flourish. Each of the phases is explained more fully below. The essence of distal mentoring is governed by an infusion of fresh ideological and practical safeguards into the constituent features of the developmental phases with particular emphasis on pre-model matching, training and mentor self-care.

The inclusion of self-care requirements for the mentor – through training, development and supervision – balances care provision within the dyad, compensating for the sustained focus on mentee care in each phase of the model and avoiding the negative chronic repercussions of toxicity on the mentor (such as a reluctance to continue mentoring). This approach could improve mentoring scheme success, develop staff more effectively and ultimately protect the organisation's investment.

The concept of this model reflects the transition of power in the relationship from mentor to mentee within a cross professional, cross organisational environment. The matrix in Figure 4 marks the mentoring activity taking place in each phase. While this implies a distinctive demarcation of function, in reality it is less clear-cut with boundaries fusing inconspicuously. Scenarios have been included to illustrate the working of each phase, followed by relevant excerpts from mentor/mentee interviews that relate to them.

The model emphasises the reinforcing role of emotional intelligence and the transition of power in the relationship between mentor and mentee. It also underlines the significance of mentor self-care and the final section of this chapter has been devoted entirely to this frequently glossed-over issue.

Figure 4:   DISTAL MENTORING MODEL

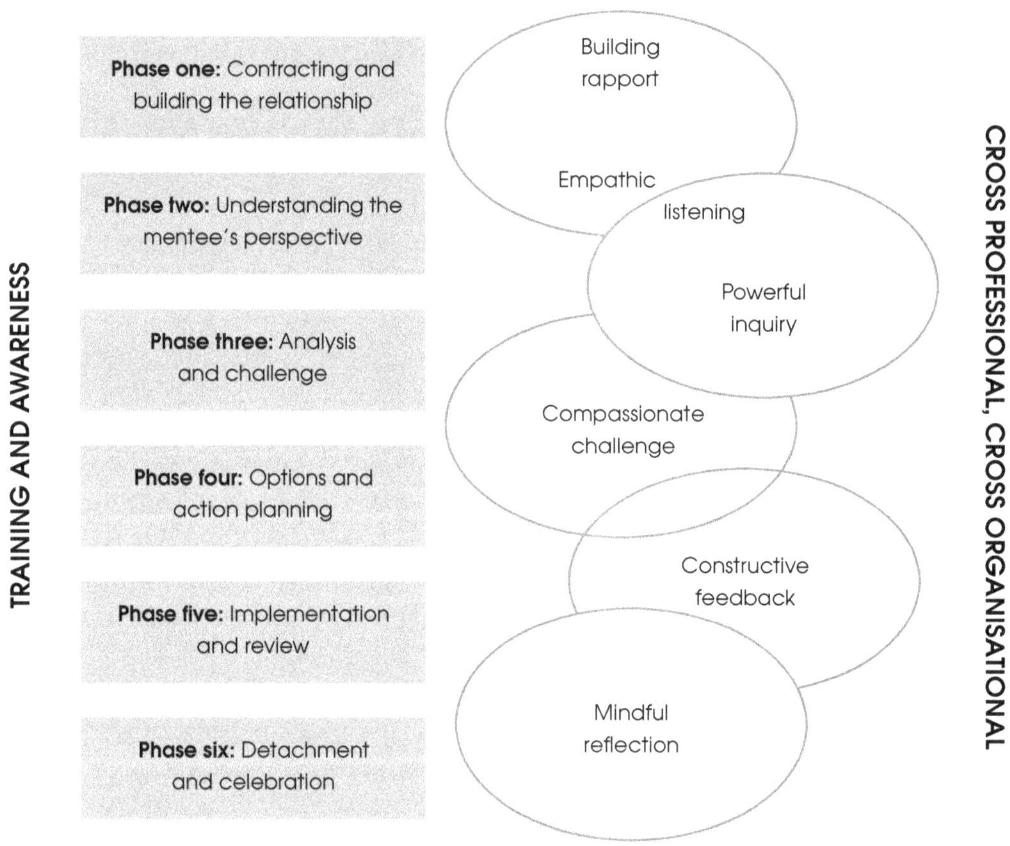

TRAINING AND AWARENESS

Phase one: Contracting and building the relationship

Phase two: Understanding the mentee's perspective

Phase three: Analysis and challenge

Phase four: Options and action planning

Phase five: Implementation and review

Phase six: Detachment and celebration

Building rapport

Empathic listening

Powerful inquiry

Compassionate challenge

Constructive feedback

Mindful reflection

CROSS PROFESSIONAL, CROSS ORGANISATIONAL

As the distal model incorporates many facets from existing models, the following portrayal of its phases should be read in conjunction with chapter 5 (Mentoring Schemes) which explains in greater detail the processes and ideals promoted:

a)   Phase one: contracting and building the relationship
This opening phase establishes the viability of the relationship. It seeks to establish value alignment, respect and agreement of purpose. Finding mutual accord through exploration of ground rules, boundaries and expectations helps to create a closer rapport, fuelling the trust so essential if the mentee is to fully share and confide during the process. Successful rapport creation can be checked through confirmation indicators: verbal and non-verbal signs such as eye contact and body language. Several should be sought out to confirm rapport creation.

The focus of this phase is on creating a format for preliminary meetings and incorporates the contractual elements of the relationship such as ground rules and expectations. This clarification aims to eliminate the risk of toxicity by preventing misunderstanding of roles or misalignment of expectations. Comprehensive contracting is vital for securing successful outcomes and many reviews of toxicity have identified it as a significant contribution to prevention (Johnson and Ridley, 2008). The adoption of appropriate communication avenues and the use of non-verbal behaviours, together with mentor and mentee self-disclosure, allows the dyad to establish an open, unambiguous alliance that bonds fellowship and instils trust. The key skill for the mentor during this phase is rapport building.

The dyad should work collaboratively to determine their preferred communication approaches in order to accumulate an understanding of how this may benefit the mentoring relationship. The whole process could be resolved as early as the initial meeting or it may require several sessions before the contract is successfully agreed. Ideally, the mentee will have volunteered for the process and be committed to it, but in the event of a referral the mentor will need to 'sell' the benefits to gain sufficient commitment for the process to move forward. Once rapport has been established the phase naturally evolves into a strong, trust-based dyad and bilateral mentoring agreement. The contract may also be revisited in later phases to either review or reinvigorate the relationship.

Phase one scenario: correcting a misalignment of expectations; agreeing a contract between Ginny (mentor) and Peter (mentee)

Peter has been referred for mentoring by his manager Rosie who finds him disengaged at work. Ginny and Peter are meeting for the first time and Ginny has explained her approach to mentoring, her background and experience and why she feels it can be a helpful activity.

> *Ginny:* I would like now, if it's OK with you Peter, to establish what you would like to achieve through our time together.
> *Peter:* Frankly I don't know; Rosie arranged this and I have no idea why, I don't see the point.
> *Ginny:* OK, well, it may help if I can understand more about your work.

Peter explains his job and the department, Ginny demonstrates empathic listening, saying little apart from occasionally paraphrasing to establish clarity and understanding. As Peter continues in the non-judgemental environment his apparent resentment subsides and he relaxes. At this point Ginny is able to introduce the subject of his relationship with Rosie.

> *Ginny:* So, it sounds to me that there may be some tensions in your relationship with Rosie?
> *Peter:* She never makes a decision straight away. She always seems to block me when I want to get on, and it is incredibly frustrating. I just give up now.
> *Ginny:* I think we could spend our time together exploring how you and Rosie communicate; there are a number of techniques we can use to identify her communication style and how you can manage it and therefore improve the relationship. Do you feel that would be useful to you?

Peter agrees and they spend the next few sessions employing a variety of tools and models to reflect upon communication. Using Honey and Mumford's learning styles they first establish that Rosie is likely to be a Reflector, reluctant to embrace action without first giving due consideration and quiet contemplation. Peter discovers he is a classic Activist: a sharp communicator, valuing speed and action. They go on to consider a range of theories: Belbin's team roles, to identify the strengths and weaknesses they bring; Berne's Ego States to recognise the emotional roles into which they fit. This reveals that Rosie is an Implementer, an effective organiser, but can be slow to respond to new ideas. Peter, faced by what he believes is Rosie's resistance, plays out his ego state as Adapted Child (see chapter 2). Ultimately acknowledging their differences leads Peter to adjust his communication style improving his work situation and learns in the process to appreciate the value of mentoring.

Reflection: In this scenario the mentor's first task is to disconnect the mentee from their hostility so they can discuss the issue dispassionately. Then, by using their knowledge and experience, the mentee can be led to a clearer insight into both their situation and themselves.

b) Phase two: understanding

The aim of the second phase is to acquire a deeper understanding of the mentee, establishing his/her current situation and their goals for the future. The mentor, utilising verbal and non-verbal signals, invites the mentee to express themselves in more specific terms whilst respecting their opinions and providing feedback. Rapport building matures during this stage and is particularly pertinent when exploring values and motivation as the mentee reveals more of their story.

A common gambit for this 'getting to know you' stage is to perform a 'stocktake' of the mentee's context, circumstances, strengths and opportunities to construct a broader picture.

For example, asking the mentee to talk about:

- their workplace
- the organisation
- their colleagues
- their role and how it fits
- what they are good at
- where and how they might like to improve

This routine interplay stimulates a supportive and encouraging environment that can strengthen the relationship and trust within the partnership as well as providing the opportunity of revelation and self-discovery for the mentee. Mentor skills include deep, non-judgemental listening and empathy to ensure the mentee feels understood, offering them validation and congruence.

Empathic listening skills can reveal underlying feelings hidden in the subconscious that may not initially be obvious to the mentee. They are, however, enabled through the process to take stock of their situation and review issues of experience, skills, and personal circumstances within the organisational context. It can identify if an issue emanates from within the mentee (feelings), or outside the mentee (circumstance). Areas open to exploration can include current role priorities, career history and the future, and often leads on to clarify the ultimate purpose of the collaboration. Depending on the nature of the issues raised and the depth of reflection required, the phase may occupy more than one session.

Having dealt with the more practical arrangements and ground rules, this next step enters the realm of deepening the relationship through mutual understanding and empathy. Feelings that surface during this phase can be powerful and, on rare occasions, may prove disturbing for the mentee. Even where competency boundaries have been settled in the earlier phase, the mentoring session can still risk slipping into a counselling activity leading to a situation that the mentor is unprepared for or unqualified to facilitate. It demonstrates the importance of establishing professional and competency boundaries.

Phase two scenario: an uncomfortable conversation; Rhys (mentor) and Oscar (mentee) talk about Oscar's increasing unhappiness at work

> *Rhys:* Oscar, in our last session we discussed ways to help you be more involved and engaged with your job to get more out of it, and you were going to reflect on that. How are you feeling now?
> *Oscar:* Not so good; it just seems pointless, all of it. I fell out with Megan again, she's been covering for me, I keep getting in late and last week I went down the pub at lunchtime and I just didn't return.

Rhys notices that this is the third reference to the pub Oscar has made and suspects there may be a problem, possibly with alcohol and perhaps depression.

> *Rhys:* Do you go to the pub every day now? Didn't you only go on Fridays?
> *Oscar:* So?
> *Rhys:* And you seem to stay longer and longer there. Didn't you mention Megan covering for you before too?
> *Oscar:* I know; she has been really good. I know I can't go on like this.
> *Rhys:* I think it is really good, Oscar, that you recognise there is a problem and while I'd like to continue to see you, I think it may be useful for some additional support. Would you consider meeting with the firm's counsellor, Isaac? I think he could really help you to deal with this current situation and enable us to continue to work on your engagement.

Reflection: Rhys, upon recognising that there may be deeper psychological issues facing Oscar, wisely chooses to signpost to professional help. He will continue to mentor Oscar through his difficulties if only to keep in touch until he is ready to focus on his career again. This recognition of the boundaries of his own competence will mean that their mentoring relationship can continue and even be strengthened through adversity.

c) Phase three
The analysis and challenge phase provides the platform for mutual learning as the mentee broadens their insight and the mentor challenges any discrepancies in self-perception that may be impacting on confidence. Harvesting this deeper understanding within the dyad opens the way for the desired shift of power from mentor to mentee.

Both parties need to work as a team to monitor and assess progress, reaching a higher level of awareness and deeper understanding that acknowledges the mentee's leading role in events. The ability of the mentor, through the use of empathic listening techniques and powerful inquiry, is directed at stimulating within the mentee a sense of being fully understood and empathised with. The mentor may deliver an impression of expertise, even where none exists, by being politically astute even though it is the mentee in possession of the technical know-how. These contrasting inputs do not impede the collaboration, allowing the dyad to address issues as partners, each recognising the other's contribution. The mentor will use skills to create an environment of trust allowing the mentee to speak freely, encouraging a creative milieu for the mentee to develop solutions and explore ideas which fully recognise their expertise. Non-judgemental, empathic listening and powerful inquiry can unlock rigid perceptions sufficiently to allow alternative options or solutions to be considered.

The direction of mentor behaviour may alter from being passive in the second phase to being more openly challenging in the third where it is deemed appropriate. Applying this change of approach is not always an obvious judgement. Adopting a more passive style when the mentee clearly needs guidance and advice could impede momentum, and a badly-timed directive approach could prevent the mentee's contribution to the analysis, potentially disempowering them. The ability to 'read' a mentee's progress is a particularly useful skill for the mentor and comes more easily as understanding of the mentee grows. Any misjudgement can however be easily rectified by taking a step back or a readjustment of the approach.

The purpose of this third phase is to explore issues in greater depth, encouraging frankness, and to bridge any gaps or contradictions in perceptions. A number of devices are available to the mentor to facilitate this process including listening and reflecting, questioning, empathy, and self-disclosure models such as Johari's Window (Luft et al., 1955). Other beneficial tools include Lifelines and SWOT analysis (strength, weaknesses, opportunities, threats). Hamlin and Sage's (2011: 768) lay model of positive mentor behaviours proposed compiling a mentor's 'toolkit' from various models and techniques to support the mentee. Underpinning the use of these aids with mentoring strategies such as powerful inquiry serves to inspire the mentee to generate their own solutions.

Phase three scenario: Alfie steps back to view the big picture; Megan (mentor) guides Alfie (mentee) through a lifeline

> *Megan:* Last time Alfie, you agreed to draw a lifeline for me noting the significant events in your career.

Alfie produces a road map diagram, identifying his first job, promotions and important life events such as the birth of his son. Megan invites Alfie to talk her through these events.

> *Alfie:* I was so excited to receive my first promotion; it made me even more determined to get to the next step and being successful in my career has taken priority. But when my son, Jack, was born it felt like my whole world shifted; he is

the most important thing in my life and it made me want to be even more successful, for him.
Megan: How old is he?
Alfie: Well, he is nearly five now. That time has gone so quickly. Look, I've had three more promotions in that time! I suppose it's been a very successful five years. It's only now, looking at this picture, that I realise it's come at a cost. Those promotions were tough. I had to work really hard for them; late nights, early mornings, weekends. I can't remember the last time I read my boy a bedtime story, like my Dad did for me.
Megan: Maybe it's time to re-evaluate your priorities and think about how that could work for you.

Reflection: Stepping back from your life with a mentor can help to clarify your next steps.

d) Phase four

The options and action planning phase lies at the heart of the collaboration and involves identifying opportunities, making reasoned choices and planning their execution. It is preferable to consider a range of options which can emanate from either party although the mentee is encouraged to lead the process by introducing some initial suggestions. The mentor can stimulate this by challenging the mentee to shift perspectives. For example, if the mentee is struggling to manage a challenging work relationship, it may be helpful to encourage them to first consider the problem from their colleague's perspective through the use of role play.

The process could also involve the use of other techniques such as:

- *Brainstorming:* where all potential ideas regardless of their practicality are generated.
- *Force field analysis:* where alternatives and consequences are investigated.
- *Scenario planning:* where a course of action considered most likely to succeed is acted out.
- *Option appraisal:* where a detailed evaluation of each option is undertaken.
- *Visual pathways:* where different pathways are literally drawn to trace possible outcomes.
- *Resource identification:* identifying who and what is needed to succeed.
- *Contingency planning:* where alternatives are plotted in case of disappointment.

The mentee's own ideas usually surpass those of the mentor, fully justifying the case for holding back interventions.

Phase four scenario: selecting an option; Ginny (mentor) and Peter (mentee) agree an action

> *Ginny:* In our last session you were considering the best way forward for your career. Have you now made a decision?
> *Peter:* I have. As we agreed, I discussed things with Rosie – who I'm getting on much better with – and she is encouraging me to go for promotion.
> *Ginny:* That's really positive, well done.
> *Peter:* I'm just a bit worried about the interview. Rosie won't actually be on the panel and I'm feeling nervous about the whole thing.
> *Ginny:* Well, the more prepared you are the less nervous you may feel. We could discuss the interview process and what sort of things might be discussed, and if we use contingency planning we can prepare a range of responses so that you can feel confident whatever they ask you.

Reflection: Peter enthusiastically agrees and together they consider the job role, predict a range of questions and role play answers for Peter to increase his confidence.

e)   Phase five

Review and implementation is where the mentee sets in motion the action plan settled on in phase four followed by an examination of the outcome. Implementation secures autonomy and responsibility for the mentee's own development. The relationship moves from the mentor-driven influences through skills, such as empathic listening and challenge, to mentee-centred behaviour, where the mentee determines potential solutions for themselves rather than being directed to them by the mentor. The mentor's awareness and judgement in applying the appropriate mentoring style, from clarification to solutions, is vital to secure a satisfactory conclusion. By leading the implementation process, the mentee is fulfilling the relationship transformation at the heart of the distal model.

Mutual feedback, while encouraged throughout the relationship, is particularly relevant at this stage. Feedback must be motivated by a reciprocal desire to learn. The mentor should avoid representing themselves as a teacher but instead seek a team approach, offer feedback in a constructive and nurturing way and invite feedback on themselves to allow the mentee to develop this vital and easily misunderstood skill. The distal mentoring model aligns with Egan's (2014) 'just society'. This is based on Smaby and Tamminen's (1979) concept of relationships founded on mutual respect and shared planning, with the model's refinement empowering the mentee with responsibility.

This feedback is highly relevant to the review element of this phase. If implementation is successful it provides an opportunity to consider what has been learnt and how it can be built upon. While it is desirable to get things right first time, the review process is even more important in the event of an implementation failure. The mentor's role is to respond non-judgementally, rebuild confidence and seek the positives before identifying what went wrong, how it could be changed and the best way to try again. Edison, after all, discovered many ways how not to make a light bulb before finding the right one.

The mentor should also conduct a review of their own input and, aided by mentee feedback, clarify, in hindsight, whether it worked well or if other options may have been more appropriate. This constant re-evaluation inevitably improves future performance.

Phase five can be aptly described as the outcome of the mentoring process. The two stages: implementation of the action plan and review of the results, culminates in a decision to either re-contract or end the process.

Phase five scenario: reviewing the relationship; Ginny (mentor) and Peter (mentee) review their long-standing ten month mentoring relationship

> *Ginny:* Firstly, I'd like to congratulate you on your promotion. Well done!
> *Peter:* Thanks and I really appreciate all your help; these meetings have boosted my confidence and helped with my strategic awareness of the business and that really helped at the interview.
> *Ginny:* Well, we have achieved what we set out to do, so we need to talk about what happens next but first I'd really like to review what we've achieved together.

Reflection: Ginny and Peter discussed their meetings from initial contracting, through the early meetings where Peter was uncommunicative and Ginny struggled to engage him until they discovered a mutual interest in psychometrics which led to the use of a variety of tools in their interactions. Ginny asked for feedback on these early, more challenging meetings with regard to her mentoring style and Peter explained that he would have benefitted, at that point, from a more direct approach. Ginny thanked him for this useful feedback and they continued to recount some of the barriers and opportunities they discovered together. They finished by acknowledging the success of the relationship and the part they both played in it.

f) Phase six: detachment and celebration.
The final phase may require a fundamental change in direction for the partnership or signal the end of the association. The distal model encourages recognition, review and celebration of the relationship before moving on. Unresolved endings can cause toxicity, particularly for the mentee. Discussion on how to end the relationship should be held at the contracting stage to eliminate uncertainty. Successful endings therefore link to the initial contracting phase with the cyclical nature of distal mentoring preparing the dyad from the outset for the ending of the relationship, or guiding a shift in focus for the dyad's continuation.

The very nature of mentoring can create intense relationships and a strong bond within the dyad. Abrupt endings can cause feelings of loss, especially for the mentee. By this stage the mentor should be aware of the mentee's disposition and ability to handle closure and therefore the level of sensitivity that needs to be adopted. Celebrating achievements and the progress of the mentee and guiding them to acknowledge the end of the process psychologically softens the outcome.

Phase six scenario: ending the relationship; Rhys (mentor) helps Oscar (mentee) to end their mentoring relationship and move on.

> *Rhys:* Now we have reviewed our mentoring relationship and given each other feedback – by the way, thank you for that as I found it really useful – I think it is time to close the process. If you recall in our contracting discussions when we first met we talked about the importance of closing the relationship and celebrating what we've achieved together.
> *Oscar:* Yes, this has made such a difference to me; you encouraged me to get help from Isaac and his counselling has helped me manage my drinking so much. Then when we resumed our meetings you really helped me to repair my relationship with Megan. I feel like my career is back on track again which is amazing. I just feel a little anxious that we won't be meeting again.
> *Rhys:* You have done so well and it has been such a pleasure to work with you. If you think about our last few sessions, you've been taking the lead, coming up with ideas and strategies. You have the capability to continue from strength to strength but, if it would help you, you can always contact me for a one-off discussion, or indeed if you would like to re-establish the relationship with a different focus.

Reflection: Oscar did not continue the relationship but did have one, short follow-up meeting to ease him back. Knowing that he had Rhys as a resource gave him the confidence to trust in himself and strengthened his own resilience and self-belief.

Overview
The final phases encompass the true intent of distal mentoring: the empowerment of the mentee to assume full responsibility for their own development. The facilitative style required to inspire the mentee necessitates shrewd judgement on the part of the mentor.

The distal model emphasises the importance of contracting and using empathic skills, and this pragmatic approach to mentoring is similar to that adopted by Mullen and Schunk's (2012) utilisation of the initiation phase of Kram's four phase model which embraces connection and groundwork. The empathic skills are akin to those used in Carnell, MacDonald and Askew's (2006) learning-centred conversation: active listening, open questioning and being non-judgemental. The distal model generally encompasses recommended best practice and while not specifically designed to address toxicity, many of its elements are recognised as doing so.

The distal model of mentoring is a practical, technique-focused concept. Phases one and two, utilising specific skills such as rapport building are believed to be significant in the prevention of toxicity. Any scheme utilising the model should endeavour to provide appropriate training that focuses on contracting to establish clear expectations and trust, the skills utilised during the relationship, such as empathic listening, and the importance of ending the relationship clearly and positively.

The concept of network support and mentoring outside the organisation is a fundamental aspect of distal mentoring, with the detachment of the mentor and the organisation offering greater confidentiality to the mentee.

Mentor/mentee reflections

The extracts in Table 7 share views expressed by participants during the study and may serve to illuminate some of the concepts outlined in this chapter.

Table 7: STUDY PARTICIPANT EXTRACTS

Phase one: contracting and building the relationship	'I think both parties need to know what mentoring is, what I expect from you, what you expect from me and what you want to get out of it, even if it means we're not really the right people for each other. I think the ground rules, exploring all the factors at the beginning of the relationship is beneficial.'
	'What I found really good about the training was it makes you think, mentoring is sometimes an add-on, you don't really get the time to think about how its set up, and I think the Scheme helps you to think about what it looks like and to remind you about the boundaries and issues, I think it encourages you.'
Phase two: understanding the mentee's perspective	'Another thing is "knowing" your mentee, I always do a series of tests, I tell them about it on the first meeting, so I do a Belbin's role test, see what sort of role they have, I do the Honey and Mumford learning cycle. I can adapt to them and that's the only reason I do that. If I know they're more an activist rather than a reflector then they need more action learning, where a reflector would need to think more about things. I find that helps the more you know about your mentee, understand how they think, which is why it is good to be prepared, it only takes 10 minutes to read up so you can go in prepared.'

Phase three: analysis and challenge	'The good point about the Scheme was that it gave me lots of handholds in terms of thinking about my life and how my character and everything impacted on other people and vice versa. So I got to understand myself.' 'I think that all mentoring relationships should be outside of your comfort zone.'
Phase four: options and action planning	'I think it did open my eyes. It certainly made me think about how you need to keep your mouth shut to find the resonance for the other side. It's very easy to do all the talking or create your own solutions. I think you gave me an understanding of how difficult it is to mentor and mentor well.'
Phase five: review and implementation	'I think there is a partnership approach to it, the review opportunity for the mentee to feedback how they feel and that they feel they can say, you've started to take over the session, that opportunity.'
Phase six: detachment and celebration.	'I do think it is important to have a degree of formality from the outset so that you've got an agreed set of expectations. Even though it is a formal relationship in the sense that somebody is providing expertise for the other person, it almost feels like breaking a friendship over time and that is awkward. Whereas you can go back to the contract in a more formal way.'

Mentor self-care

The participatory nature of distal mentoring extends beyond style and skills and into the roles themselves. Mentor and mentee share equal importance in the dyad and therefore the well-being of both is essential to a successful outcome. While the mentee's welfare must always be the central concern, the mentor is often overlooked. Johnson and Ridley (2008: 107) urge long-term mentors to 'consistently practice self-care', in order to protect their physical and emotional well-being. They advise that personal commitments should be honoured as much as fulfilling mentee obligations. There is little research on mentor self-care per se, although it has been noted as an almost incidental sideline in other research – self-care for psychologists who mentor (Johnson, 2002), for example. Keep (2011), in her study of self-care in coaching, found that few coaches allow for personal well-being in their professional practice.

Self-awareness in terms of mentoring is very much associated with emotional intelligence and resilience but it tends to be scrutinised more from the perspective of the mentee or the dyad. While some supervision does exist to support mentors through development and trouble-shooting (Megginson et al., 2006), the focus remains on their practice and, indirectly, the mentee as a consequence. However, some professions, such as coaching, do recognise, to some extent, that lack of self-care can affect the relationship (Hawkins, 2010).

Failure to self-care is akin to self-harm and a bit like riding a motorcycle without a crash helmet – fine until you get knocked off. Incidents of a complete 'crash' are thankfully rare and the actuality is more of an insidious 'creep' with the symptoms often going unnoticed at the onset. The implications can be significant, eroding resilience and threatening mentor consistency or even a transference of negativity to the mentee, i.e. toxic!

Chronic negative effects may also discourage mentors from future participation, particularly significant for voluntary schemes. Safeguards, such as supervision, self-applied resilience techniques, or greater awareness through reflection, need to be employed as precautionary measures against toxicity.

Guide to mentor self-care

Recognising emotional overload or burnout is not always obvious particularly if you are the one experiencing it. The signs include:

- exhaustion due to disturbed sleep patterns, where even the simplest task seems to require an inordinate amount of effort and concentration
- losing your sparkle: everything met with a lack of enthusiasm and diminished self-motivation
- frustration: feeling every change is a hindrance thwarting you
- ineffectiveness: lack of energy or motivation to move forward; the lack of progress leaves you with feelings of failure

The following tactics can all serve as preventative or restorative measures but more crucially aid cognisance of impending problems:

- *Seek supervision*
  Supervision is being mentored on your mentoring: exploring techniques, discussing ethical issues, to reflect on problems and to provide emotional backup. Supervision is often practiced in groups with a facilitator. It is particularly useful for sharing good practice and serves as a consultancy to focus on a particular issue, approach or technique, allowing the whole group to develop as mentors. Apart from its problem-solving purpose, it acts as a reflective space with others contributing their own expertise and experience. It also guards against isolation, burnout and provides a celebration of what you do. Mentoring is usually a voluntary activity and supervision should be regarded as a reward for your service. If there is no convenient group available to you, organise your own regular supervisory meetings to create a mentoring network of joint support. Invite experts in the field to guest at your meetings; you will be surprised how many will happily attend free of charge.

That, after all, lies at the heart of mentoring where financial rewards should play no part.

- *Become a mentee*
  Mentors invariably witness the beneficial effects of engagement with their mentees so it is self-evident that a mentor's mentor can induce similar results. This form of peer mentoring represents one of the best sounding boards for personal appraisal, working through personal issues or bolstering self-confidence. Being a mentee enables a confidential, independent and dependable assessment of our psychological well-being in its potential to give early warning of negative influences and, by addressing them, reinvigorate interest and energise performance. Experiencing how other mentors operate conveys the added advantage of understanding your mentee's perspective and it can improve your own mentor practice.

- *Self-reflection*
  Scheduled self-reflection following each session allows time and space to consider your mentoring session. Review the questions you asked and the way you listened. Reflect on how your mentee reacted to the session and how that response affected you. If it did not go well ask yourself how you could better help your mentee next time, what other approaches or skills you could use or what other help you may need. Addressing these questions as preparation for the next meeting reduces any anxiety about how that session may turn out.

- *Emotional self-regulation and resilience*
  Mentoring can be draining and it is important to refill emotionally, finding a leeway from a mentoring session back into routine life. It is also necessary to recognise the difference between a simple need for some emotional respite from when you are in need of outside help. Physical and emotional well-being can be protected by undertaking a regular assessment against a checklist of criteria you have established when in good health. Identify acceptable levels then check to see if you meet them, and if not, have a plan to address it. For example, physical changes such as weight gain or mental fragility (such as the inability to make decisions) are warnings to take heed and make some time for yourself.

- *Self-mentor*
  You are in possession of all the skills needed to support yourself; try using them as if you were a mentee and mentor yourself accordingly, applying the same compassion and respect. It is vital to give yourself permission to look after yourself, not only for your own welfare but also for the care of anyone you are mentoring. This should form

an integral part of mentoring practice. Advise yourself, spend time with friends and family or simply do whatever makes you feel good.

- *Practice self-compassion*
  We tend to be hardest on ourselves, and giving the inner critic full voice is particularly unhelpful when we need self-care. Regard yourself as vulnerable and imperfect and in need of kindness and care. When we are at a low ebb and someone shows us kindness it is uplifting, so practice and utilise this simple and potent technique to quash the inner critic. We are all more effective when we feel good about ourselves.

Scenario: Ginny practices self-care

Ginny prided herself on her ability to cope: juggling a demanding job, a young family and a busy household. She also made time for her mentoring activities, appreciating the pleasure and sense of achievement this gave her when helping others. However, recently she noticed her sleep patterns altering; she fell asleep easily but was waking earlier and unable to return to sleep so started her day unrested. Ginny recognised this as a possible warning of emotional overload and stepped back to take stock of her situation. She realised that work had been particularly demanding with her assistant, Olivia, away on long-term absence resulting in longer hours and increased workload. This had caused her to miss her daughter's school play which she still felt unhappy and guilty about. She was also supporting a mentee experiencing stress at work but facing debt problems that she was unqualified to deal with, and she felt uncertain how to proceed.

Ginny suspected that his financial problems may have created referred stress so first signposted her mentee to the organisation's staff service to help him manage his debts before tackling his work-related stress. She met with her manager and requested temporary support until her assistant returned. She forgave herself for missing her daughter's play and arranged to spend regular time with her. Once she started to take positive action her sleep patterns improved.

Reflection: Taking a few positive steps to address problem issues is often sufficient to relieve anxiety even where the final resolution takes some time. Seeing the light at the end of the tunnel can prove quite uplifting. Even when you emerge from it to find another tunnel ahead, taking them as one obstacle at a time avoids small problems merging to form a large one.

Summary

Distal mentoring implies a relationship transformation over a period of time but it also alludes to its co-participatory nature, using skills such as powerful inquiry to elicit mentee contribution and ensure a team association with equal division of power. It places the onus of listening on the mentor rather than providing instant advice, while the mentee is encouraged to explore and create solutions. Consequently, the mentor has no need of specialised knowledge in the mentee's field or profession. This approach provides the opportunity for evolving mentoring as a field. The implications for the profession are potentially significant, extending access to mentoring by increasing the pool of mentors. The absence of the need for specialist knowledge creates a non-judgemental mentoring experience, offering opportunities for cross mentoring. This bridges the professions, organisations, public and private sector, injecting differing perspectives to enrich the process.

> **CHAPTER TIPS**
>
> Using the six phases of the distal mentoring model in conjunction with the skills building blocks and self-care for mentors offers a complete and comprehensive structure for your mentoring scheme. Operating cross-organisationally opens up the pool of mentors and increases confidentiality. The challenge is the cross-professional aspect and yet this can be the most powerful. Mentees inherently believe they require an expert in their field to mentor them. This is partly due to lack of self-confidence and the belief that they need to be instructed. However, mentoring conversations usually focus not on the specifics of a job but on universal concepts such as self-belief, managing relationships and understanding communication. Ask a mentee what the issue is and once you brush away the dressing of the circumstance you will find the basic, boiled-down ingredients: fear, jealousy, ambition, confidence, acceptance, values. We have a basic need to feel fulfilled in our work, to make a contribution, to feel valued; distal mentoring in its entirety can help attain this.

Afterword

The central theme for The Mentor's Companion has been on the value of mentoring in optimising organisational potential through the personal growth of its workforce, but mentoring also contributes significantly to the customised development of our distinctive selves. As it is the 'whole' person that comes to work, the work/life connection is reciprocal.

As a person-centred activity, mentoring has the capacity to help define our true self by making us more intuitive. It is ideal for breaking stereotypical moulds or unshackling restrictive conformity to re-write your life script into something more appealing to you. It also enables us to replace impulse with considered thought, better deal with emotions and strengthen resilience. Achieving a goal is not always the final act of the story. It may be that the end result is not as expected, in which case mentoring can soften disappointments and encourage us to re-evaluate and choose another path.

Understanding ourselves represents a big step towards unlocking the repressed subconscious, freeing ourselves from what Jung called 'the shadow self'. Lying within the unconscious, inaccessible to the conscious mind, the shadow self represents elements that the conscious mind does not identify with. The subconscious level, more easily accessible once our attention is drawn to it, lies between the two and can translate information from the unconscious. Mentoring can help us to engage with what the subconscious can tell us, allowing us to challenge unwanted underlying traits such as pessimism.

The emphasis on empathy provides a vehicle for understanding other points of view, helping us to remove or put aside biases. It also serves to highlight the uniqueness of individuals. What research has shown is that different people react differently to similar situations and that difference can be quite marked. Mentoring therefore demands a personalised and responsive approach, with a mentor able to read the signs. Things can occasionally go wrong and the health and safety of the mentee is paramount. These toxic threats can, however, be significantly reduced by applying the structures and principles outlined in this book.

If, as a would-be mentor, you have doubts, put them aside and take the plunge. Or, as a seasoned mentor, you feel that you know it all, open your mind and heart to learning; you may be surprised. Good mentoring is like baking a cake, it first requires a recipe. Understanding yourself through striving to become more mindful, empathic and emotionally intelligent, source the necessary ingredients for a stable mentoring attitude. Success also demands the skill of a chef, and blending such techniques as empathic listening and powerful inquiry will improve mentoring outcomes. Bear in mind you will not become cordon-bleu overnight, it takes practice, reflection and commitment.

Mentoring serves all levels of society. It can create an elite but is not elitist and is just as effective for remodelling the dysfunctional into the functional, or simply getting the very best out of ourselves.

The motivation to mentor suggests an altruistic nature
The desire to consistently reflect, question, challenge and enhance mentoring skills
Indicates a true Mentor

References

Allen, T. D., 'Mentoring Relationships from the Perspective of the Mentor', in B. R. Ragins and K. E. Kram (eds) *The Handbook of Mentoring at Work Theory, Research and Practice* (California: Sage, 2007), pp. 123–48

Allen, T. D., L. T. Eby, M. L. Poteet, E. Lentz and L. Lima, 'Career Benefits Associated with Mentoring for Protégés: A Meta-Analysis', *Journal of Applied Psychology*, 89 (2004), 127–36

Allen, T. D. and L. M. Finkelstein and M. L. Poteet, *Designing Workplace Mentoring Programs: An Evidence-Based Approach* (West Sussex: Wiley-Blackwell, 2012)

Armstrong, A. R., R. F. Galligan and C. R. Critchley, 'Emotional intelligence and psychological resilience to negative life events', *Personality and Individual Differences*, 51/3 (2011), 331–6

Arora, R. and S. Rangnekar, 'Workplace Mentoring and Career Resilience: An Empirical Test', *The Psychologist-Manager Journal*, 17/3 (2014), 205–20

Beech, N. and A. Brockbank, 'Power/Knowledge and Psychosocial Dynamics in Mentoring', *Management Learning*, 30/1 (1999), 7–25

Berne, E., *Games people play: the psychology of human relationships* (London: Andre Deutsch, 1966)

Berne, E., *Intuition and Ego States* (California: TA Press, 1977)

Bloom, B. S. and D. R. Krathwohl, D. R., *Taxonomy of Educational Objectives: The Classification of Educational Goals, by a committee of college and university examiners* Handbook I: Cognitive Domain. (New York: Longmans, Green, 1956)

Boud, D., R. Keough and D. Walker, D., *Reflection: Turning experience into Learning* (London: Kogan Page, 1985)

Boyatzis, R. E., 'Mentoring for Intentional Behavioural Change', in B. R. Ragins and K. E. Kram (eds) *The Handbook of Mentoring at Work Theory, Research and Practice* (California: Sage, 2007), pp. 447–70

Brockback, A. and I. McGill, *Facilitating Reflective Learning Through Mentoring and Coaching* (London: Kogan Page, 2006)

Bush, J., A. Adam and R. Saunders, 'Are mentors necessary for success?', *The International Journal of Mentoring*, 4/2 (1992), 33–9

Campbell, T. A. and D. E. Campbell, 'Outcomes of mentoring at-risk college students: gender and ethnic matching effects', *Mentoring and Tutoring: Partnership in Learning*, 15/2 (2007), 135–48

Carnell, E., J. MacDonald and S. Askew, *Coaching and Mentoring in Higher Education: A learning-centred approach* (London: Institute of Education, 2006)

Cherniss, C., 'The Role of Emotional Intelligence in the Mentoring Process', in B. R. Ragins and K. E. Kram (eds), *The Handbook of Mentoring at Work Theory, Research and Practice* (California: Sage, 2007), pp. 427–46

Clutterbuck, D., *Everyone Needs a Mentor, Fostering talent in your organisation*, 4th edition (London: CIPD, 2004)

Coffield, F., D. Moseley, E. Hall and E. Eccleston, *Learning styles and pedagogy in post-16 learning: a systematic and critical review* (London: Learning & Skills Research Centre, 2004)

Colky, D. L. and W. H. Young, 'Mentoring in the virtual organisation: keys to building successful schools and businesses', *Mentoring and Tutoring*, 14/4 (2006), 433–47

Coll, J. and P. Raghavan, 'Mentoring: Who and How', *Journal of College Teaching and Learning*, 1/8 (2011), 65–78

Colley, H., 'A Rough Guide to the History of Mentoring from a Marxist feminist perspective', *Journal of Education for Teaching International research and pedagogy*, 28/3 (2002), 257–73

Colley, H., 'Engagement mentoring for 'disaffected' youth: a new model of mentoring for social inclusion', *British Education Research*, 29/4 (2003), 505–26

Connor, M. and J. Pokora, *Coaching and Mentoring at Work, Developing Effective Practice* (New York: Open University Press, 2007)

Copeland, L. and N. Peck Beins, 'A Resilience Model for School-Based Mentoring Programs', *Journal of Border Educational Research*, 4/2 (2005), 47–52

Cox, E., 'For better, for worse: the matching process in formal mentoring schemes', *Mentoring and Tutoring*, 13/3 (2005), 403–14

Cox, E., *Coaching Understood, a pragmatic inquiry into the coaching process* (London: Sage, 2013)

Daloz, L. A., *Mentor: Guiding the Journey of Adult Learners* (California: Jossey-Bass, 1999)

Department for Education and Skills, Children's Plan (2007), *www.dfes.gov.uk/publications/the-childrens-plan*

Eby, L. T., 'Understanding Relational Problems in Mentoring', in B. R. Ragins and K. E. Kram (eds), *The Handbook of Mentoring at Work Theory, Research and Practice* (California: Sage, 2007), pp. 323-44

Eby, L. T. and T. D. Allen, 'Further investigation of protégés negative mentoring experiences: Patterns and outcomes', *Group and Organization Management*, 27 (2002), 456-79

Eby, L. T., M. Butts, J. Durley and B. R. Ragins, 'Are bad experiences stronger than good ones in mentoring relationships? Evidence from the protégé and mentor perspective', *Journal of Vocational Behavior*, 77/1 (2010), 81-92

Eby, L. T., J. R. Durley, S. C. Evans and B. R. Ragins, 'Mentors' perceptions of negative mentoring experiences: Scale development and nomological validation', *Journal of Applied Psychology*, 93/2 (2008), 358-73

Eby, L. T. and A. Lockwood, 'Protégés and mentors' reactions to participating in formal mentoring programs: A qualitative investigation', *Journal of Vocational Behavior*, 67 (2005), 441-58

Eby, L. T. and S. E. McManus, 'The protégés role in negative mentoring experiences', *Journal of Vocational Behavior*, 65 (2004), 255-75

Eby, L. T., S. E. McManus, S. A. Simon and J. E. A. Russell, 'The Protégé's Perspective Regarding Negative Mentoring Experiences: The Development of a Taxonomy', *Journal of Vocational Behavior*, 57 (2000), 1-21

Egan, G., *The Skilled Helper a problem-management and opportunity-development approach to helping*, 10th edition (CA: Brooks/Cole Cengage Learning, 2014)

Ensher, E. A. and S. E. Murphy, 'Effects of race, gender, perceived similarity, and contact on mentor relationships', *Journal of Vocational Behaviour*, 50/3 (1997), 460-81

Ensher, E. A., C. Thomas and S. E. Murphy, 'Comparison of Traditional, Step-Ahead, and Peer Mentoring on Protégés' Support, Satisfaction, and Perceptions of Career Success: A Social Exchange Perspective', *Journal of Business and Psychology*, 15/3 (2001), 420

European Commission, transnational good practice (2007), ec.europa.eu/research/science-society/document_library/pdf_06/structural-changes-final-report_en.pdf

Everard, K. B. and G. Morris, G., *Effective School Management*, 4th edition (London: Paul Chapman Publishing Ltd., 2004)

Feldman, D. C., 'Toxic mentors or toxic protégés? A critical re-examination of dysfunctional mentoring', *Human Resource Management Review*, 9/3 (1999), 247-78

Fleck, C. and M. E. Mullins, 'Evaluating a Psychology Graduate Student Peer Mentoring Program', *Mentoring and Tutoring: Partnership in Learning*, 20/2 (2012), 271-90

Furnham, A. and K. V. Petrides, 'Trait Emotional Intelligence and Happiness', *Social Behavior and Personality: an international journal*, 31/8 (2003), 815-23

Garvey, B., 'Mentoring in a Coaching World', in E. Cox, T. Bachkirova and D. Clutterbuck (eds), *The Complete Handbook of Coaching – Developmental Coaching* (London: Sage, 2010), pp. 341–54

Gaskell, C., *HR directors will gain if line managers will take on coaching* (2007), connection.ebscohost.com/c/editorials/24897941/hr-directors-will-gain-if-line-managers-take-coaching

Goleman, D., *Emotional Intelligence: why it can matter more than IQ* (London: Bloomsbury, 1996)

Görgens-Ekermans, G. and T. Brand, 'Emotional intelligence as a moderator in the stress-burnout relationship: a questionnaire study on nurses', *Journal of Clinical Nursing*, 21:15/16 (2012), 2275–85

Grant, A. M., 'The impact of life coaching on goal attainment, metacognition and mental health', *Social Behaviour and Personality*, 3/3 (2003), 253–63

Hamlin, R. G. and L. Sage, 'Behavioural criteria of perceived mentoring effectiveness an empirical study of effective and ineffective mentor and mentee behaviour within formal mentoring relationships', *Journal of European Industrial Training*, 35/8 (2011), 752–78

Hargreaves, E., 'Knowledge construction and personal relationship: Insights about a UK university mentoring and coaching service', *Mentoring & Tutoring: Partnership in Learning*, 18/2 (2010), 107–20

Harvard Business Essentials, *Coaching and Mentoring: How to Develop Top Talent and Achieve Stronger Performance* (Boston: Harvard Business School Publishing, 2004)

Hawkins, P., 'Coaching Supervision', in E. Cox, T. Bachkirova and D. Clutterbuck (eds), *The Complete Handbook of Coaching* (London: Sage, 2010), pp. 381–93

Hay, J., *Transformational Mentoring: Creating developmental alliances for changing organisational cultures* (Watford: Sherwood Publishing, 1995)

Higgins, M. C., D. E. Chandler and K. E. Kram, 'Developmental Initiation and Developmental Networks', in B. R. Ragins and K. E. Kram (eds), *The Handbook of Mentoring at Work Theory, Research and Practice* (California: Sage, 2007), pp. 349–72

Høigaard, R and P. Mathisen, 'Benefits of formal mentoring for female leaders', *International Journal of Evidence Based Coaching and Mentoring*, 7/2 (2009), 64–70

Honey, P., *People: the missing link in e-learning*, The Coaching and Mentoring (2007) www.coachingnetwork.org.uk/information-portal/Articles/ViewArticle.asp?artID=50

Honey, P. and A. Mumford, A., *The manual of learning styles* (Maidenhead: Peter Honey Publications, 1982)

Irby, B. J., 'Editor's overview: Defining developmental relationships in mentoring for mentor/mentee dyads, for mentors and for mentoring programs', *Mentoring & Tutoring: Partnership in Learning*, 21/4 (2013), 333–7

Johannessen, B. G. G., *Global Co-Mentoring in Higher Education* (Springer International Publishing, 2016)

Johnson, W. B., 'The intentional mentor: Strategies and guidelines for the practice of mentoring', *Professional Psychology: Research and Practice*, 33/1 (2002), 88–96

Johnson, W. B., and C. R. Ridley, *The Elements of Mentoring* (New York: Palgrave Macmillan, 2008)

Karpman, S. B., 'Fairy tales and script drama analysis', *Transactional Analysis Bulletin*, 7/26 (1968), 39–43

Kao, K-Y., A. Rogers, C. Spitzmueller, M-T. Lin and C-H. Lin, 'Who should serve as my mentor? The effects of mentor's gender and supervisory status on resilience in mentoring relationship', *Journal of Vocational Behavior*, 85 (2014), 191–203

Keep, J., *Developing Self-Care for Coaches*, EMCC UK 4th Annual Coaching and Mentoring Conference 29–30 March PhD study presentation (2011), www.eprints.uwe.ac.uk/21799/1/Phd%20Study%20Jane%20Keep%2012102013%20Final.pdf

Kennett, P. and T. Lomas, 'Making meaning through mentoring: Mentors finding fulfilment at work through self-determination and self-reflection', *International Journal of Evidence Based Coaching and Mentoring*, 13/2 (2015), 29–44

Kent, A. M., F. Kochan and A. M. Green, 'Culture influences on mentoring programs and relationships: a critical review of research', *International Journal of Mentoring and Coaching in Education*, 2/3 (2013), 204–17

Kram, K. E., 'Phases of the mentor relationship', *Academy of Management Journal*, 26/4 (1983), 608–25

Kram, K. E., *Mentoring at work: Developmental relationships in organisational life* (Illinois: Scott Foresman, 1985)

Learning Wales, Coaching and Mentoring Information Booklet (2015) www.learning.gov.wales/docs/learningwales/publications/150313-coaching-and-mentoring-en-pdf

Latham, G. P., E. A. Locke and N. E. Fassina, N. E., 'The high performance cycle: Standing the test of time', *Psychological management of individual performance*, (2012), 201–28

Lee, G., 'The Psychodynamic Approach to Coaching', in E. Cox, R. Bachkirova and D. Clutterbuck (eds), *The Complete Handbook of Coaching* (London: Sage, 2010), pp. 23–36

Luft, J., and H. Ingham, *The Johari window, a graphic model of interpersonal awareness, proceedings of the western training laboratory in group development* (California: UCLA, 1955)

Maslow, A., 'A theory of human motivation', in D. Buchanan and A. Huczynski (eds), *Organizational behaviours: integrated readings* (Hemel Hempstead: Prentice Hall, 1997), pp. 45–61

McGovern, J., M. Lindemann, M. A. Vergara, S. Murphy, L. Barker and R. Warrenfeltz, 'Maximizing the Impact of Executive Coaching: Behavioural Change, Organizational Outcomes, and Return on Investment', *The Manchester Review*, 6/1 (2001), 1–9

McManus, S. E. and J. E. A. Russell, 'Peer Mentoring Relationships', in B. R. Ragins and K. E. Kram (eds) *The Handbook of Mentoring at Work Theory, Research and Practice* (California: Sage, 2007), pp. 273–98

Megginson, D. and D. Clutterbuck, *Techniques for coaching and mentoring* (Oxford: Butterworth Heinemann, 2005)

Megginson, D., D. Clutterbuck, B. Garvey, P. Stokes and R. Garrett-Harris, *Mentoring in Action: a practical guide* (London: Kogan, 2006)

Metropolitan Police, *Metropolitan Police Service and Metropolitan Police Authority Joint Annual Report 2004/5,* MPS/MPA, (2004), 44

Mullen, C.A. and D. H. Schunk, 'Operationalizing Phases of Mentoring Relationships', in S. J. Fletcher and C. A. Mullen (eds) *The SAGE Handbook of Mentoring and Coaching in Education* (London: Sage, 2012), p. 89

Murray, M., *Beyond the myths and magic of mentoring: How to facilitate an effective mentoring process* (San Francisco: Jossey-Bass, 2001)

Parker, M. A., 'Mentoring Practices to Keep Teachers', *School International Journal of Evidence Based Coaching and Mentoring*, 8/2 (2010), 111–23

Parsloe, E. and M. Leedham, *Coaching and Mentoring Practical Conversations to improve learning* (London: Kogan Page, 2009)

Pascarelli, J., 'A Four-Stage Mentoring Model that Works', in *Mentoring and Tutoring by Students*, S. Goodlad (ed.) (London: Kogan Page Ltd, 1998), pp. 231–243

Pegg, M., *The Art of Mentoring* (Cirencester: Management Books 2000 Ltd, 1999)

Pryce-Jones, J., *Happiness at Work: Maximizing Your Psychological Capital For Success* (Chichester: Wiley-Blackwell, 2010)

Rolfe, A., *Mentoring: Mindset, Skills and Tools* (Mentoring Works, 2012)

Scandura, T. A. and R. Viator, R., 'Mentoring in public accounting firms: an analysis of mentor-protégé relationships, mentoring functions, and protégé turnover intentions', *Accounting, Organizations and Society*, 19 (1994), 717–34

Seligman, M. E. P. and M. Csikszentmihalyi, 'Special issue: Positive psychology', *American Psychologist*, 55/1 (2000)

Simon, S. A. and L. T. Eby, 'A Typology of Negative Mentoring Experiences: A Multidimensional Scaling Study', *Human Relations*, 56/9 (2003), 1083–1106

Smaby, M. and A. W. Tamminen, 'Can we help belligerent counselees?', *Personnel and Guidance Journal*, 57 (1979), 506–12

Tugade, M. M. and B. L. Fredrickson, 'Resilient Individuals Use Positive Emotions to Bounce Back From Negative Emotional Experiences', *Journal of Personality and Social Psychology*, 86/2 (2004), 320–33

Wallace, S. and J. Gravells, *Professional Development in the Lifelong Learning Sector Mentoring*, 2nd edition (Exeter: Learning Matters Ltd, 2007)

Washington, R., 'Distal mentoring: An antidote to toxicity?', *International Journal of Evidence Based Coaching and Mentoring*, Special Issue No. 7 (2013), 73-81

Washington, R., 'Developmental Mentoring in the Workplace: Delivering the Promise', in Hill, Hudson, Mckendry, Raven, Saunders, Storan and Ward (eds), *Closing the Gap: Bridges for Access and Lifelong Learning* (London: Forum for Access and Continuing Education, 2016), pp. 55-72

Washington, R. and E. Cox, 'How an Evolution View of Workplace Mentoring Relationships Helps Avoid Negative Experiences: The Developmental Relationship Mentoring Model', *Mentoring & Tutoring: Partnership in Learning*, 24/4 (2016), 318-40

Wells, C., Mindfulness *How School Leaders Can Reduce Stress and Thrive on the Job* (Maryland: Rowman & Littlefield, 2016)

WUMS, *Women in Universities Mentoring Scheme* (2010) www.wums.southwales.ac.uk/wums/background/

Zachary, L. J., *The Mentor's Guide: Facilitating effective learning relationships* (CA: John Wiley & Sons, 2012)

Bibliography

Alexander, G., 'Behavioural coaching – the GROW model', in J. Passmore (ed.), *Excellence in coaching: The Industry Guide* (Philadelphia: Kogan Page, 2006), pp. 83–94

Allen, T. D. and L. T. Eby, 'Factors related to mentor reports of mentoring functions provided: gender and relational characteristics', *Sex Roles*, 50 (1) (2004), 129–39

Allen, T. D. and M. L. Poteet, 'Developing effective mentoring relationships: strategies from the mentor's viewpoint', *The Career Development Quarterly*, 48/1 (1999), 59–73

Alred, G., B. Garvey and R. Smith, *Mentoring Pocketbook* (Hants: Management Pocket Books, 1998)

Ashwin, P., 'Implementing Peer Learning Across Organisations: the development of a model', *Mentoring & Tutoring*, 10/3 (2002), 221–31

Askew, S. and C. Lodge, 'Gifts, ping-pong and loops – linking feedback and learning', in S. Askew (ed.), *Feedback for Learning* (London: Routledge Falmer, 2000), pp. 1–17

Bandura, A., 'Self-efficacy', in V. S. Ramachaudran (ed.), *Encyclopedia of human behavior* (New York: Academic Press, 1994), pp. 71–81

Baugh, S. G. and E. A. Fagenson-Eland, 'Boundaryless Mentoring: An Exploratory Study of the Functions Provided by Internal Versus External Organizational Mentors', *Journal of Applied Social Psychology*, 35/5 (2006), 939–55.

Beck, J. S., *Cognitive Therapy for Challenging Problems: what to do when the basics don't work* (New York: The Guildford Press, 2005)

Belbin, M., *The Management of Teams: Why they succeed or fail* (Burlington: Elsevier, 1981)

Bell, A., 'Looking for Professor Right: mentee selection of mentors in a formal mentoring program', *Higher Education*, 61/5 (2011), 545–61

Bennetts, C., 'Traditional mentor relationships, intimacy, and emotional intelligence', *International Journal of Qualitative Studies in Education*, 15 (2002), 155–70

Blake-Beard, S. D., R. M. O'Neill and E. M. McGowan, 'Blind Dates? The Importance of matching in Successful Formal Mentoring Relationships', in B. R. Ragins and K. E. Kram (eds), *The Handbook of Mentoring at Work Theory, Research and Practice* (California: Sage, 2007), pp. 617-32

Bolton, G., *Reflective practice, Writing and professional development* (London: Paul Chapman Publishing Ltd, 2001)

Boud, D., R. Keough and D. Walker, *Reflection: Turning experience into Learning* (London: Kogan Page, 1985)

Bozionelos, N., G. Bozionelos, K. Kostopoulos, and P. Polychroniou, 'How providing mentoring relates to career success and organizational commitment: A study in the general managerial population', *Career Development International*, 16/5 (2011), 446-68

Brechtel, M. F., cited in Cherniss, C., 'The Role of Emotional Intelligence in the Mentoring Process', in Ragins, B. R. and Kram, K. E. (eds), *The Handbook of Mentoring at Work Theory, Research and Practice* (California: Sage, 2004), pp. 427-46

Brockback, A. and I. McGill, *Facilitating Reflective Learning Through Mentoring and Coaching* (London: Kogan Page, 2006)

Bush, J., A. Adam, and R. Saunders, 'Are mentors necessary for success?', *The International Journal of Mentoring*, 4/2 (1992), 33-9

Cavanagh, M. J. and A. M. Grant, 'The Solution-focused Approach to Coaching', in E. Cox, T. Bachkirova and D. Clutterbuck (eds), *The Complete Handbook of Coaching* (London: SAGE, 2010), pp. 54-67

Chao, G. T., 'Formal mentoring: Lessons learned from past practice', *Professional Psychology: Research and Practice*, 40/3 (2009), 314-20

Coates, W. C., 'Being a Mentor: What's in it for Me?', *Academic Emergency Medicine*, 19/1 (2012), pp. 92-7

Colley, H., *Mentoring for Social Inclusion a critical approach to nurturing mentor relationships* (London: Routledge Falmer, 2004)

Connor, M. P., A. G. Bynoe, N. Redfern, J. Pokora, J. Clarke, 'Developing senior doctors as mentors: a form of continuing professional development. Report of an initiative to develop a network of senior doctors as mentors: 1994-99', *Medical Education*, 34/9 (2000), pp. 747-53

Cowan, C. A., E. F. Goldman and M. Hook, 'Flexible and inexpensive: Improving learning transfer and program evaluation through participant action plans', *Performance Improvement*, 49/5 (2010), 18-25

Cox, E. and P. Jackson, 'Developmental Coaching', in E. Cox, T. Bachkirova and D. Clutterbuck (eds), *The Complete Handbook of Coaching - Developmental Coaching* (London: Sage, 2010), pp. 217-30

Cull, J., 'Mentoring young entrepreneurs: what leads to success?', *International Journal of Evidence Based Coaching and Mentoring*, 4/2 (2006), 8-18

Dancer, J. M., 'Mentoring in healthcare: theory in search of practice?' *Clinician in Management*, 12/1 (2003), 21–31

Darling, L., 'What do Nurses Want in a Mentor?' *Journal of Nursing Administration*, 14/10 (1984), 42–4

Davenport, J. and J. Early, 'The Power-Influence Dynamics in a Consultant/Client Relationship', *Journal of Financial Service Professionals*, 64/1 (2010), 72–5

Day, A., E. D. De Haan, E. Blass, C. Sills and C. Bertie, 'Coaches' experience of critical moments in the coaching', *International Coaching Psychology Review*, 3/3 (2008), 207–18

Eby, L. T., J. R. Durley, S. C. Evans and B. R. Ragins, 'The relationship between short-term mentoring benefits and long-term mentoring outcomes', *Journal of Vocational Behavior*, 69/3 (2006), 424–44

Eliahoo, R., 'Meeting the potential for mentoring in Initial Teacher Education: mentors' perspectives from the Lifelong Learning Sector', *Teaching in lifelong learning: a journal to inform and improve practice*, 1/2 (2009), 64–75

Elliott, C., J. D. Leck, B. Orser and C. Mossop, 'An Exploration of Gender and Trust in Mentoring Relationships', *Journal of Diversity Management*, 1/1 (2011), 1–12

Ensher, E. A. and S. E. Murphy, *Power Mentoring: How successful mentors and protégés get the most out of their relationships* (California: Jossey-Bass, 2005)

Ensher, E. A. and S. E. Murphy, 'The Mentoring Relationship Challenges Scale: The impact of mentoring stage, type and gender', *Journal of Vocational Behavior*, 79/1 (2011), 253–66

Figley, 'Compassion Fatigue: Psychotherapists' Chronic Lack of Self Care', *Journal of Clinical Psychology*, 58/11 (2002), 1433–41

Fletcher, J. K. and B. R. Ragins, 'Stone Center Relational Cultural Theory', in B. R. Ragins and K. E. Kram (eds), *The Handbook of Mentoring at Work Theory, Research and Practice* (California: Sage, 2007), pp. 373–400

Freedman, M., *The Kindness of Strangers: Reflections on the Mentoring Movement* (Philadelphia: Public/Private Ventures, 1991)

Garvey, B., 'When mentoring goes wrong', in D. Clutterbuck and G. Lane (eds), *The Situational Mentor: An International Review of Competencies and Capabilities in Mentoring* (Hants: Gower, 2004), p. 173

Godshalk, V. M. and J. J. Sosik, 'Aiming for career success: The role of learning goal orientation in mentoring relationships', *Journal of Vocational Behavior*, 63/3 (2003), 417–37

Goleman, D., *Working with emotional intelligence* (London: Bloomsbury, 1998)

Grant, A. M. and M. J. Cavanagh, 'Life Coaching', in E. Cox, T. Bachkirova and D. Clutterbuck (eds), *The Complete Handbook of Coaching – Developmental Coaching* (London: Sage, 2010), pp. 297–310

Gray, D. E. and H. Goregaokar, 'Choosing an executive coach: The influence of gender on the coach-coachee matching process', *Management Learning*, 41/5 (2010), 525–44

Gray, M. A. and L. N. Smith, 'The qualities of an effective mentor from the student nurse's perspective: findings from a longitudinal qualitative study', *Journal of Advanced Nursing*, 32/6 (2000), 1542–9

Greenhaus, J. H. and R. Singh, 'Mentoring and the Work-Family Interface', in B. R. Ragins, and K. E. Kram (eds), *The Handbook of Mentoring at Work, Theory, Research and Practice* (California: Sage, 2007), pp. 519–44

Goodlad, S., *Students as tutors and mentors* (London: Kogan Page, 1995)

Goodlad, S. and T. B. Hirst, *Peer Tutoring – A Guide to Learning by Teaching* (London: Kogan Page, 1989)

Haggard, D. L., 'Mentoring and Psychological Contract Breach', *Journal of Business and Psychology*, 27/2 (2012), 161–75

Haggard, D. L., T. W. Dougherty, D. B. Turban and J. E. Wilbanks, 'Who Is a Mentor? A Review of Evolving Definitions and Implications for Research', *Journal of Management*, 37/1 (2011), 280–304

Hale, M. M., 'Mentoring Women in Organizations: Practice in Search of Theory', *The American Review of Public Administration*, 25/4 (1995), 327–39

Hamilton, R., *Mentoring* (London: The Industrial Society, 1993)

Hansford, B., L. Tennent and L. C. Elrich, 'Business Mentoring: help or hindrance?', *Mentoring and Tutoring*, 10/2 (2002), 101–15

Hargreaves, A. and M. Fullan 'Mentoring in the new millennium', *Theory into Practice*, Volume 39/1 (2000), 50–6

Harper, A., 'psychometric tests are now a multi-million pound business: what lies behind a coach's decision to use them?', *International Journal of Evidence Based Coaching and Mentoring*, 2 (2008), 40–51

Harrington, S., 'Mentoring new nurse practitioners to accelerate their development as primary care providers: A literature review', *Journal of the American Academy of Nurse Practitioners*, 23/4 (2011), 168–174

Hart, V., J. Blattner, and S. Leipsic, 'Coaching versus therapy: A perspective', *Consulting Psychology Journal: Practice and Research*, 53/4 (2001), 229–37

Harvey, M., N. McIntyre, J. Thompson Heames and M. Moeller, 'Mentoring global female managers in the global marketplace: traditional, reverse and reciprocal mentoring', *The International Journal of Human Resource Management*, 20/6 (2009), 1344–61

Hawkey, K., 'Emotional intelligence and mentoring in pre-service teacher education: a literature review', *Mentoring & Tutoring*, 14/2 (2006), 137–47

Hay, J., *Working it Out at Work: Understanding Attitudes and Building Relationships* (Watford: Sherwood Publishing, 2009)

Hay, J., 'Developmental mentoring: Creating a healthy organisational culture', *Journal of Communication Management*, 4:4 (2013), 378–84

Holbeche, L., 'Peer mentoring: the challenges and opportunities', *Career Development International*, 1/7 (1996), 24–7

Homer, *The Odyssey*, trans. R. Fagles (London: Penguin, 1997)

Huskins, W. C., K. Silet, A. M. Weber-Main, M. D. Begg, V. G. Fowler, J. Hamilton and M. Fleming, 'Identifying and Aligning Expectations in a Mentoring Relationship', *Clinical and Translational Science*, 4/6 (2011), 439–47

de Janasz, S. C., S. E. Sullivan and V. Whiting, 'Mentor networks and career success: Lessons for turbulent times', *Academy of Management Executive*, 17/4 (2003), 78–91

Johnson, P. and J. Duberley, *Understanding management research: an introduction to epistemology* (London: SAGE, 2011)

Jones, G. and K. Spooner, 'Coaching High Achievers', *Consulting Psychology Journal Practice and Research*, 58/1 (2006), 40–50

Jones, R. and D. Brown, 'The Mentoring Relationship as a Complex Adaptive System: Finding a Model for Our Experience', *Mentoring and Tutoring*, 19/4 (2011), 401–18

Kahn, J. S. and R. M. Greenblatt, 'Mentoring early-career scientists for HIV research careers', *Journal Information*, 99/1 (2009), S7–S42

Kalbfleisch, P. J., 'Mentoring Enactment Theory: Describing, Explaining, and Predicting Communication in Mentoring Relationships', in B. R. Ragins, B.R. and K. E. Kram (eds), *The Handbook of Mentoring at Work Theory, Research and Practice* (California: Sage, 2007), pp. 499–518

Karcher, M. J., G. P. Kuperminc, S. G. Portwood, C. L. Sipe and A. S. Taylor, 'Mentoring Programs: A Framework To Inform Program Development, Research, And Evaluation', *Journal of Community Psychology*, 34/6 (2006), 709–25

Kauffman, C., I. Boniwell and J. Silberman, 'The Positive Psychology Approach to Coaching', in E. Cox, T. Bachkirova and D. Clutterbuck (eds), *The Complete Handbook of Coaching – Developmental Coaching* (London: Sage, 2010), pp. 158–71

Kay, D. and R. Hinds, *A Practical Guide to Mentoring how to help others achieve their goals* (Oxford: How to Books, 2009)

Kerr, S. and S. Landauer, 'Using stretch goals to promote organizational effectiveness and personal growth: General Electric and Goldman Sachs', *The Academy of Management Executive*, 18/4 (2004), 134–8

Kilburg, G. M., 'Three mentoring team relationships and obstacles encountered: a school-based case study', *Mentoring and Tutoring; Partnership in Learning*, 15/3 (2007), 293–308

Kilburg, G. M. and T. Hancock, 'Addressing Sources of Collateral Damage in Four Mentoring Programs', *Teachers College Record*, 108/7 (2006), 1321–38

Klasen, N., *Implementing Mentoring Schemes A practical guide to successful programs* (Oxford: Elsevier, 2002)

Lankau, M. J. and T. A. Scandura, 'Mentoring as a Forum for Personal Learning in Organizations', in B. R. Ragins and K. E. Kram (eds), *The Handbook of Mentoring at Work Theory, Research and Practice* (California: Sage, 2007), pp. 95–122

Lecornu, R., 'Peer mentoring: engaging pre-service teachers in mentoring one another', *Mentoring and Tutoring*, 13/3 (2005), 355–66

Lewis, G., *The Mentoring Manager – strategies for fostering talent and spreading knowledge* (London: Pitman Publishing, 1996)

Liang, B., A. J. Tracy, C. A. Taylor and L. M. Williams, 'Mentoring College-Age Women: A Relational Approach American', *Journal of Community Psychology*, 30/2 (2002), 271–88

Liu, H., R. Macintyre and R. Ferguson, 'Exploring Qualitative Analytics for E-Mentoring Relationships Building in an Online Social Learning Environment In', *Proceedings of the 2nd International Conference on Learning Analytics and Knowledge*, ACM (2012), 179–83

Maloney, M. E., 'Ethical mentorship: the dilemma of success of failure', *Clinics in Dermatology*, 30/2 (2012), 210–15

Marcinkus Murphy, W., 'Reverse mentoring at work: Fostering cross-generational learning and developing millennial leaders', *Human Resource Management*, 51/4 (2012), 549–73

Martin, S. M. and S. K. Sifers, 'An evaluation of factors leading to mentor satisfaction with the mentoring relationship', *Children and Youth Services Review*, 34/5 (2012), 940–5

Maxwell, J. C., *Mentor 101: What Every Leader Needs to Know* (Tennessee: Thomas Nelson, 2008)

McCauley, C. D. and V. A. Guthrie, 'Designing Relationships for Learning Into Leader Development Programs', in B. R. Ragins and K. E. Kram (eds), *The Handbook of Mentoring at Work Theory, Research and Practice* (California: Sage, 2007), pp. 573–92

Moberg D. J. and M. Velasquez, 'The ethics of mentoring', *Business Ethics Quarterly*, 14/1 (2004), 95–122

Moss, P., K. J. Debres, A. Cravey, J. Hyndman, K. K. Hirschboeck and M. Masucci, 'Toward Mentoring as Feminist Praxis: Strategies for ourselves and others', *Journal of Geography in Higher Education*, 23/3 (1999), 413–27

Mueller, S., 'Electronic mentoring as an example for the use of information and communications technology in engineering education', *European Journal of Engineering Education*, 29/1 (2004), 53–63

Mullen, C. and S. A. Forbes, 'Untenured faculty: issues of transition, adjustment, and mentorship', *Mentoring and Tutoring*, 8/1 (2000), 31–46

Myers, I. B., *Introduction to type: A description of the theory and applications of the Myers-Briggs Type Indicator* (California: Consulting Psychologists Press, 1987)

Neimeyer, G. and R. A. Neimeyer, 'Personal Constructs in Relationship Deterioration: A Longitudinal Study', *Social Behaviour and Personality*, 14/2 (1986), 253–7

Newton, T. and R. Napper, 'Transactional Analysis and Coaching', in E. Cox, T. Bachkirova and D. Clutterbuck (eds), *The Complete Handbook of Coaching* (London: Sage, 2010), pp. 172–86

O'Brien, K. E., A. Biga, S. R. Kessler and T. D. Allen, 'A Meta-Analytic Investigation of Gender Differences', *Mentoring Journal of Management*, 36 (2010), 537–54

O'Neill, R. M. and D. Sankowsky, 'The Caligula Phenomenon Mentoring Relationships and Theoretical Abuse', *Journal of Management Inquiry*, 10/3 (2001), 206–16

Ragins, B. R., 'Diversified mentoring relationships in organizations: a power perspective', *Academy of Management Review*, 22 (1997), 482–521

Ragins, B. R., and J. L. Cotton, 'Mentor functions and outcomes: a comparison of men and women in formal and informal mentoring relationships', *Journal of Applied Psychology*, 84 (1999), 529–50

Ragins, B. R., 'Positive Identities in Action: A Model of Mentoring Self-Structures and the Motivation to Mentor', in L. Morgan Roberts and J. E. Dutton (eds), *Exploring positive identities and organizations: building a theoretical and Research Foundation* (New York: Psychology Press, 2009), pp. 237–64

Ragins, B. R., 'Relational Mentoring: A Positive Approach to Mentoring at Work', in K. Cameron and G. Spreitzer (eds), *The Handbook of Positive Organizational Scholarship* (New York: Oxford University Press, 2010), pp. 519–36

Ragins, B. R., J. L. Cotton and J. S. Miller, 'Marginal Mentoring: The Effects of Type of Mentor, Quality of Relationship and Program Design on Work and Career Attitudes', *Academy of Management Journal*, 43/6 (2000), 1177–94

Ragins, B. R. and A. K. Verbos, 'Positive relationships in action: relational mentoring and mentoring schemas in the workplace', in J. E. Dutton and B. R. Ragins (eds), *Exploring positive relationships at work: Building a theoretical and research foundation* (New Jersey: Lawrence Erlbaum Associates, 2007), pp. 91–116

Saffold, F., 'Increasing Self-Efficacy Through Mentoring', *Academic Exchange Quarterly*, 9/4 (2005), 13–16

Scandura, T. A., 'Dysfunctional Mentoring Relationships and Outcomes', *Journal of Management*, 24/3 (1998), 449–67

Schutte, N. S., J. M. Malouff, M. Simunek, J. McKenley and S. Hollander, 'Characteristic emotional intelligence and emotional well-being', *Cognition & Emotion*, 16/6 (2002), 769–85

Slaski, M. and S. Cartwright, 'Emotional intelligence training and its implications for stress, health and performance', *Stress and Health*, 19/4 (2003), 233–9

Sosik, J. J. and V. M. Godshalk, 'Examining gender similarity and mentor's supervisory status in mentoring relationships', *Mentoring and Tutoring*, 13/1 (2005), 39–52

Spencer, R., '"It's Not What I Expected" A Qualitative Study of Youth Mentoring Relationship Failures', *Journal of Adolescent Research*, 22/4 (2007), 331–54

Standing, M., 'Developing a supportive/challenging and reflective/competency education (SCARCE) mentoring model and discussing its relevance to nurse education', *Mentoring and tutoring: Partnership in Learning*, 6/3 (1999), 3–17

Steven, A., J. Oxley and W. G. Fleming, 'Mentoring for NHS Doctors: perceived benefits across the personal-professional interface', *Journal of the Royal Society of Medicine*, 101/11 (2008), 552–7

Tenner, E., 'The Pitfalls of academic mentorships', *Chronicle of Higher Education*, 50/49 (2004), B7–B10

Tepper, B. J., 'Upward influence tactics in supervisory mentoring and non mentoring relationships', *Academy of Management Journal*, 38 (1995), 1191–1205

Terrion, J., R. Philion and D. Leonard, 'An evaluation of a peer-mentoring training programme', *International Journal of Evidence Based Coaching and Mentoring*, 5/1 (2007), 42–57

Tomlinson, P., *Understanding mentoring* (Buckingham: Open University Press, 2001)

Turban, D. B. and F. K. Lee, 'The Role of Personality in Mentoring Relationships', in B. R. Ragins and K. E. Kram (eds), *The Handbook of Mentoring at Work Theory, Research and Practice* (California: Sage, 2007), pp. 21–50

Underhill, C. M., 'The effectiveness of mentoring programs in corporate settings: a meta-analytical review of the literature', *Journal of Vocational Behavior*, 68/2 (2006), 292–307

Varkey, P., A. Jatoi, A. Williams, A. Mayer, M. Ko, J. Files, J. Blair and S. Hayes, 'The positive impact of a facilitated peer mentoring program on academic skills of women faculty', *British Medical Council Medical Education*, 12/14 (2012), www.bmcmededuc.biomedcentral.com/articles/10.1186/1472-6920-12-14

Wallace, S. and J. Gravells, *Professional Development in the Lifelong Learning Sector Mentoring, 2nd edition* (Exeter: Learning Matters Ltd., 2007)

Webb, C. and P. Shakespeare, 'Judgements about mentoring relationships in nurse education', *Nurse Education Today*, 28/5 (2008), 563–71

Zeus, P., and S. Skiffington, *The Coaching At Work Toolkit* (Sydney: McGraw Hill, 2005)

Znoj, H., 'Embitterment – A larger perspective on a forgotten emotion', *Behavioral Science*, 2 (2011), 5–16

Index

A
anxiety 31, 41, 59, 99, 100
assessment 9, 10, 60, 72, 78, 79, 99

B
boundaries 30, 67, 77–9, 84, 86, 89, 90, 96
boundary violations 54, 56, 60

C
change agent 69
co-construction 20
cognitive dissonance 33
co-mentoring 5, 6
confidentiality 67, 74, 76, 79, 83, 84, 101
constructive feedback 12, 32, 33, 62
contracting 61, 74, 77, 85-87, 94–6
coordinator 66, 68, 69, 71

D
deep listening 25
developmental mentoring 10, 12, 43, 46–7, 49, 60, 83–4
distal mentoring 10, 46, 49, 83, 85–6, 93–7, 101
dysfunctional 30, 53, 106

E
ego states 20–1, 88
e-mentoring 67, 84
emotional intelligence 5, 10, 12, 14, 25, 61–2, 83, 86, 97
empathy 6, 12, 19, 20, 22, 23, 30, 46, 89, 91, 105
ethical 5, 9, 32, 68, 72, 76–7, 84, 98
ethos 5, 8, 9, 19, 23, 65, 68, 71
evaluation 65, 78–9, 92, 94
evolution 45, 80, 83
executive mentoring 5, 66

F
framework 4, 9, 40, 46–7, 61, 66, 76, 79

G
gender 9

L
leadership 6, 45, 53
learning and development 6, 46, 55
learning styles 24, 25, 88

M
manipulative behaviours 54, 56, 60
matching 8, 23–4, 60–1, 66–8, 70–1, 83, 85

mentor self-care 85–6, 97–8, 100–1
mindfulness 10, 14, 61
mirroring 19, 23–4
motivation 8–9, 11, 13, 23, 40, 56, 61, 65, 71, 73–4, 79, 89, 98

N
non-judgemental 12, 14, 20, 27, 44, 46, 88–9, 91, 94, 101

O
observation 10, 21, 30
organisational mentoring 9, 10

P
peer mentoring 4, 5, 43, 66, 70, 99
positive psychology 8, 10, 14, 15
power 8, 15, 20–1, 26, 31, 41–3, 53, 56, 86, 90
powerful question 14, 28–30, 33, 43, 47
probing 29–30
professional development 6, 12, 15, 47, 78
psychosocial 39, 43–4, 53, 72

R
rapport building 34, 46, 87, 89, 96
redefinition 40, 43
resilience 10, 12–14, 21, 33, 44, 53, 61–2, 66, 95, 97–9, 105
role model 5–7, 10, 14, 19, 25, 28, 35, 70, 72

S
self-awareness 15, 21, 24–5, 33, 97
self-efficacy 13, 22–3, 28
separation 40, 43, 54, 83
sponsorship 4, 39, 43, 46, 72, 85
succession planning 47, 66
supervision 5–6, 58, 85, 97–8

T
toxic mentee 56, 59
toxic mentor 54, 56, 59
traditional mentoring 39–40, 43–4, 56
transference 19, 54, 60, 98